The
Lies
about
Truth

Karl Renz

The Lies about Truth

Karl Renz

Edited By
Manjit Achhra

PUBLICATIONS

A Division of Maoli Media Private Limited

This is your realization,
Reality realizing itself in this lie;
a lie of separation, a lie of oneness.
Whatever you realize, whatever you experience, is a lie.
You are the liar, the absolute liar
who's lying to himself in his infinite realization.
Who else can lie himself so perfectly and believe in himself?
Only you.

KARL RENZ

That which is not expressed by speech,
But that by which speech is expressed:
Know that to be Absolute, not what people here adore.

That which is not thought by the mind,
But that by which the mind thinks:
Know that to be Absolute, not what people here adore.

That which is not seen by the eye,
But that by which the eye sees:
Know that to be Absolute, not what people here adore.

That which is not heard by the ear,
But that by which the ear hears:
Know that to be Absolute, not what people here adore.

That which is not breathed by the breath,
but that by which the breath breaths:
Know that to be Absolute, not what people here adore.

– Kena Upanishad
∽

The Lies About Truth

Copyright © 2014 Karl Renz

First Edition: October 2014

PUBLISHED BY
ZEN PUBLICATIONS
A Division of Maoli Media Private Limited

60, Juhu Supreme Shopping Centre,
Gulmohar Cross Road No. 9, JVPD Scheme,
Juhu, Mumbai 400 049. India.

Tel: +91 22 32408074
eMail: info@zenpublications.com
Website: www.zenpublications.com

Book Design: Red Sky Designs, Mumbai
Cover Image: Detail of a painting by Karl Renz

ISBN   978-93-84363-19-2

All rights reserved. No part of this book may be reproduced or transmitted in any form or by any means, electronic or mechanical, including photocopying, recording, or by any information storage and retrieval system without written permission from the author or his agents, except for the inclusion of brief quotations in a review.

Contents

The One Who Says He Knows Reality, Should Burn In Hell Forever	13
By Trying To Be The King Of The Kingdom, You Are King Doomed	36
The Final Curtain Will Never Fall	55
The Real Will Never Be Experienced By Anyone, Not Even By Itself	83
The Peace You Can Get, Peace-Off	111
I Ask You To Be The Laziest Bastard You Can Be Because That's Your Nature	139
The Experience Of Silence Is Not Silence	168
There Is No Attainment, Only Entertainment	192
The Truth You Can Experience, Is A Fake Truth	221

Other Books by Karl Renz

- A Little Bit Of Nothingness
  81 Observations On The Unnamable

- The Song of Irrelevance
  Meditation of what you are

- Heaven and Hell

- Am I - I Am

- May It Be As It Is
  The Embrace of Helplessness

- Worry and be Happy
  The Audacity of Hopelessness

- Echoes of Slience
  Avadhut Gita Revisited

- If You Wake Up, Don't Take It Personally
  Dialogues in the Presence of Arunachala

- The Myth of Enlightenment
  Seeing Through the Illusion of Separation

ACKNOWLEDGEMENT

The Publishers wish to thank
Sanjay Inamdar, Hemant Nadkarni, Amrita Hinduja
and Anjali Walsh for their invaluable help
in making this book possible.

Chapter One

The One Who Says He Knows Reality, Should Burn In Hell Forever

~

Q: When you talk about the seven levels...

K: Different ways of experiencing yourself.

Q: You say there is no hierarchy between them?

K: In concepts yes, but in reality no. From a phantom point of view, for sure there are levels. As higher you get, as higher he gets.

Q: Do these seven levels include the fantasy world?

K: It's all fantasy!

Q: I mean what we normally call fantasy...

K: What is normal and what is not?

Q: When you are day dreaming, projecting...

K: When you watch television, when you read books. [Laughter] You are now talking about the first level of relative experiences and stories and fantasies. All of this belongs to the first level, imagine!

Q: The intellect in its highest and purest level...

K: Is still the first level. In the second level, there is already no separation and there is no one who makes any separation between high and low. High and low and all the polarities are still the first level, if we talk about hierarchy at all. When we talk about the first, we talk about the differences of better and not so good and high and low and all of that. All of that belongs to the first.

Q: Having a fantasy is still intellectual?

K: Yes.

Q: That is not a very good scheme of understanding things...

K: In the first level, there is no understanding at all. There's only ignorance.

Q: You can't say every understanding is ignorance...

K: Of course I can say that. Watch me! [Laughter]

Q: Are you saying wanking is same as meeting the capital?

K: As you say. One is a higher fuck and other one is the lower fuck. [Laughter] The higher dick needs a dictionary and the lower dick does not need any dictionary.

Q: It's simply absurd...

K: All of that is in the same level.

Q: So what about the other six fucking levels?

K: In the other six, there is no fucking. There are no two.

Q: If there are no two, why do you need six levels?

K: Don't ask me; ask God why he wants to fuck himself in seven different ways. But the first level is only one where he experiences the fucking. The rest is not even fun.

Q: Dreams are also in the first level?

K: All in the first level. Whatever we can talk about, what we can name, what we can frame is all in the first.

Q: It's like there are seven compartments and you crush everything in the first and then you have six empty compartments...

K: Wherever there are things, forms and concepts are only in the first. Adyashanti talks about the 'no-thing', that's the second level. When we talk about things, we talk about the first and no-thing would be the second – the form and the formless. But we can talk about the second level only in the first level. When you are in the second, you don't talk anymore.

Q: What about the other five?

K: Imagine! The third is the pure awareness – pure light, nothing happens in it; not even nothing happens in that. The first is happening, the second is non-happening, the third is neither happening nor not-happening. Then even that what is beyond, the absolute. The first three are presence states – presence of happening, presence of non-happening and the presence of neither. Then comes the absence of all of that. That's called the Christ-state – Initiation of the one who is beyond. After that are the five, six and seven [states].

In all mysticism they have these seven levels. The first three are personal, the fourth is beyond and the five, six and seven are impersonal. The one who claims a difference between the first and the second (state) is still a personal claim. Even the awareness that is different from first and second level is personal. That's personal samadhi.

Then the impersonal starts. The last four are impersonal samadhis. From the fourth state, no one comes back because there is no one. You can only shift as a person only in the first three. And only in the first three, there is an awareness master, the oneness master and there are disciples in the first. That's the realm of master-disciple. Now you are established in the first. Then there's one who is established in the second – oneness. Then there's one who is established in the awareness. These are the differences that you can reach as a phantom because only a phantom needs to be established. In the fourth, there is no way of establishing anyone. And the same for five, six and seven because they are just results of the fourth state – no one wakes up in waking up. Then the last three states are – no one is one in oneness and no one is aware in awareness and no one is separate in separation.

Q: Like the mirror images of the first three states?

K: Yes. But all seven are dream states. That you cannot imagine! Because they are all separate to each other. As you can talk about it, you can make it different to each other.

Q: So, the awareness masters would be in which state?

K: In the third state. Awareness master needs to be in the third state, there cannot be a master in the fourth state. They claim to be in the fourth, but whoever claims to be in the fourth, is in the third. The one who claims to be in the beyond is still in the first three. Even the one who claims that – I am the unborn is still in the first three. He could even be in the first state.

Q: So, it makes no difference if I am fantasizing or writing a poem?

K: If you like. It makes a difference that's why it's in the first state. There is a difference, I don't deny that and you feel different in one way or another. But it still needs one who makes a difference of feeling one way or another. I don't deny differences, but they are all in the first state. Oneness is already the absence of differences.

The oneness master would say writing a poem or going to the toilet are not different in nature. But both is wrong... expression of life. There are only three people I read, Ramana, Nisargadatta and Ranjit who say – By being what-you-are you transcend all seven instantly. Transcending all the seven levels of differences can only be done by being what-you-cannot-not-be. Nothing else can do it. Because whatever you do is shifting between the levels. It will not make any difference because they are all unreal.

Reality does not know any difference. And for sure not seven states. It doesn't even know itself. But if you have interest in the different states, they are like carrots for the phantom. That's the way it is. And all seven are slave states. You land somewhere and then you depart again. You are the infinite traveler between the states. Nothing is good enough because none of that is permanent. They are always shifting.

Even if there would be a permanent state, it would be different to the impermanent state. So, it still would be separation. That's why they are called dream states. I like it. For me, it's fantastic! If this is as good as anything, what's the problem? Good or bad applies only when there's something better than this. If none of that is better than this, what's the problem?

The next is the next. In the first, you are the first. In the second, you are the second. And none of them makes you more or less as you are. None of them gives you the rest you are looking for because rest cannot be found and peace cannot be found and truth cannot be found in any one of them. That's called peace.

And any peace you can find – peace off! It's the same with beauty. You cannot find beauty in any one of them. Thank God beauty cannot be found. Art cannot be found. Art is what-you-are but whatever you experience is artificial. The seven possibilities are artificial possibilities of what-you-are but not the experience of art. That what is art cannot be found in one of them. That is very peaceful.

But the moment you know that there is more art than this; you are in your fucking mind of differences. Then you have to defend your insights. It's all war. If you know what is art, you have to fight for it. It's a war of what you think is better than something else. And you long for the end of war, but you will not find the end of war in all the seven states. All the seven fighting against the other. Every state is fighting against the other six, trying to be better.

The first one fights – There are only happenings here, nothing happens in other states, so stay here. This is your true place, having a body. It's boring there, so stay here. So, you even fear to go to the next state. You make sure that you stay here because you don't know what happens there. You think you may be bored and then you even fear the oneness and awareness.

Q [Another visitor]: Is keeping quiet still in the first state?

K: Who can stay there? And who can be quiet there? The answer is only the phantom 'me'. Trying to be quiet is still a misery because there is always failing. What you can experience is the absolute failure and that's called 'me'.

Q: So, all that I experience is a falsity?

K: Only for the one who claims he is real, he experiences falsity. For that what is Reality, there is neither Reality nor falsity. There's only what-you-are. There is no definer left who defines falsity. I am not talking about you becoming reality. Reality doesn't know any Reality. But you think you can know Reality by being it and by experiencing everything else as false, you again make it as a false Reality.

Q: It's another desperate attempt for suicide but it doesn't work...

K: Nothing works. You want to find a place of comfort but you cannot find one and yet you still want to create one. You want to rest and even if you find this rest, it would be a fake rest.

Q: So, there's absolute nothing that you can do?

K: You can do whatever but it doesn't matter. By none of that you attain what-you-are. And you have nothing to gain. This gaining business of the phantom, you cannot stop. You better be in spite of it what-you-are and not because of the phantom finding rest and understanding something. All that understanding, all that finding, all the losing belongs to the dream object which is what you believe to be. It's always a loser. Even gaining is losing.

Q: So, what to do?

K: Have a sip of coffee or look at him [Pointing to a visitor]. It's as good or bad as anything. It's unimaginable to look at him. [Laughter] What-you-are is witnessing everything. You have to witness that guy forever – that's hell. [Laughter]

But that is what-you-are, the Absolute witness witnessing all the states. Can you imagine that? No, you can only be that. For the almighty absolute witness, the absolute Self, it's just its nature. The nature of That is being Absolute witness and dreaming infinite witnesses witnessing what can be witnessed, in whatever possibility.

But you can never become that by any technique. But that you never lost. So, if I tell you that you are the absolute witness of Paul and whatever he does, you don't have to imagine what he's doing. [Laughing] Thank God no one needs to imagine that.

But if you ask me what you are? Then I say that story will never end. Never ending story of Reality realizing in all possible ways. And there's nothing to take. There's nothing to bear.

Q: How does it feel when one is trapped?

K: Like you now. That's how it feels to be trapped. Even that cannot be avoided by what-you-are. Even all of that is part of your infinite dream. Infinite traps, infinite trapper, infinite victims, infinite – whatever. That is Yudhisthira in hell when Krishna asks him can you take that? Is there any tendency left of avoiding that? Yudhisthira says – No, may it be as it is. In that there is no hell, no me, no devil, no Krishna. There is only That what-you-are – ever was, always will be. But even that you cannot do.

Q: The 'me' tries to avoid that?

K: Of course! The 'me' is the tendency to avoid discomfort. You want to find a place where there's only comfort, only bliss, only beauty, only what you imagine how it has to be. By the love for yourself, trying to get the best for yourself, you get the worst. That's the way it is. If you want to be in peace, you are in war. Even the good intention of peace brings war. The intention of beauty brings ugliness. The intention of rest brings restlessness.

But you cannot avoid it. You cannot avoid one intention out of that dream of intentions. So, it's very understandable that the moment you know yourself, you want to get rid of that one. The intention of suicide is there from the beginning your very first seed of longing. God knowing himself is two Gods too many. Then he wants to kill himself.

This is the suicide attempt of God. You are running now – experiencing everything. Trying to get rid of himself, by art, by intellect, by all means – he wants to get rid of experiencing himself because the moment he experiences himself, he's in trouble. It's a potential of a troubled mind, a troubled love, a passionate love for himself and that's always discomfortable. Even the possibility of separation is already discomfort. The seed of discomfort is already there in the awareness of existence. So, the false starts very early. Even the absolute potential of *Parabrahman*, is the absolute potential of falsity. Because that what you call Reality can only realize itself in falsity. It cannot otherwise realize itself. All the experiences, however profound they may seem to be, are all false. False, false, false...

But the beauty of Reality is that it doesn't need any reality to be what-it-is. And the one who says he knows Reality, he should burn in hell forever. And he will burn in hell forever. He will burn in this relative knowledge of being an owner of shit. That's already hell enough. That's why I call it owner-shit.

[A visitor coughs]

Drop dead you beast! It's the virus I mean, not the Irish. [Laughter]

Q [Another visitor]: That what you sometimes call the underwear, the Absolute...

K: People ask me why don't you call it awareness or God and I tell them I could call it underwear but it would be as not-fitting as God or Self. So, don't tell me that I call it underwear, I don't call it anything.

Q: What I just heard referred to an Absolute witness...

K: The Absolute seer, the Absolute witness... the Absolute.

Q: I seem to recognize that somehow...

K: That's quite easy for you. It's just being that. I just take all the possibilities away then you are the absolute left over: That what you cannot-not-be. So, there's an understanding beyond imagination. That understanding never needs to understand anything. That knowledge never needs to know anything. I am directly talking to That and it may happen that you recognize that because it's your natural state, your very nature which never needs anything to be what-it-is.

That's why I talk like that. I try to kill everything that can be killed. But what-you-are is life itself, it can never be killed. But everything else can be killed. All the names and forms and masters and levels can be killed. You don't have to pay attention to that, that's why it's so natural. You don't have to pay, so kill the bill. There's no bill that you have to pay. There's no karmic history that you have to work out. All of that is bullshit! So, kill the idea that you have to pay attention to anything to be what-you-are.

Q: When you are talking I recognize it immediately...

K: Of course! It's a total recognition of being it, but not by any effort. It's an effortlessness of being it but it's not that you have to make an effort and be it. It's not a result of something. It's not because of something. You are in spite of all the efforts, not because. And that's your natural state. This effortlessness cannot be claimed as 'my' effort – I did something, I am not established now in something. Whoever says I am established in something, fuck him! [Laughter] He can only be established in bullshit.

This paradox of Ramana of self-abidance is effortlessness. Just being what-you-are. But not abiding in something. The Self never needs to abide in anything to be what-it-is and that what needs to abide in something, is a beast that bites.

Now you can imagine what I try to do here, try to take all your belief system – the believer, the believing and what you believe in. *Tabula rasa*! [Blank slate] Killing what can be killed. If it would work, I would chop your head right away, but it doesn't help. I have told you the story of a Zen master where three thousand people get instantly enlightened but you never listen.

Q: I do not remember...

K: In the early times of Zen monasteries in Japan, everything could be done without any consequences. There was a Zen master and a disciple who said 'I am ready master, do whatever you like with me. I want to get enlightened, I accept everything. I am the most ready and no one was ever as ready as me'. The master calls him and asks 'Would you give your little finger for That? The disciple starts crying 'My Finger?' The master chops his little finger off. The master asks him, 'Are you less now?' Then he cuts his whole hand. The disciple cries and master asks him, 'Are you less now?' Then he cuts his whole arm and asks, 'Are you less now?' Then he chops his whole head and asks, 'Are you less now?' And there was no answer and that's what-you-are. [Laughter]

From that instant, you could ask all three thousand disciples, 'Are you enlightened?' And no one ever wanted to be enlightened. Three thousand instant enlightened disciples. Everyone was quiet.

Since we are not in those good old times, now I have to do it differently. Then it was easier, now it's really hard work. That's the meaning of Kali goes chopping with all the skeletons and the heads. That's the nature of Kali and if Kali goes chopping, watch out! Now Kali sits here and says no heads have to fall, no one has to be enlightened, all of that is same bullshit as everything.

Chopping even the chopping. That's what Ramana is famous for. That understanding will not make anything different relatively.

Ramana was the pointer of the chopping of the chopping. No chopping can ever chop that. No chopping will ever result to that you can know yourself. In that sense, there are no good old times. There's not even now for you to become what-you-are. But it sounds good, I like the story.

Q [Another visitor]: The restlessness was always there in humanity since time immemorial...

K: Since God knows himself, he is restless.

Q: When I think like this, I understand what you say...

K: Since existence exists, there's restlessness.

Q: It's very easy to think, life was very simple before...

K: [Laughing] No electricity, no plugs, no fridge, it was very simple. Working your ass off just to have a meal. Now you go to McDonalds just by the way. If it was about easy, it's easier now than it ever was for daily life. You just need to work half an hour a day for your food or less. Earlier you had to work for twelve hours a day just to get your food. In that way, it's much easier now. But people are not more satisfied by anything.

Q: Sleeping was much easier then...

K: Yeah, because you were exhausted. Now everyone is full-on and still tries to sleep. That's why work more and sleep better.

Q [Another visitor]: What is the meaning of earnestness mentioned by Nisargadatta?

K: In Bombay I found out that the word in Marathi is totally different. It means if totality decides for that to happen, it will happen. Then a translator translates that you have to be earnest. No, it actually says, if it's meant for you to happen, it will happen whether you like it or not. But then comes 'I Am That' and the translation there is all wrong. Now they listen to the tapes of what was translated and they all think – what did they translate?

But for a seeker, it sounds good because then you think I can do something. If I just would be earnest enough. I would work on my earnestness. No what he said in the tapes that if it would happen, it would happen and you cannot make it earlier or postpone anything. If it's supposed to happen, it will happen, whether you like it or not but not because of anything that you have done before. It's absolute in spite of your earnestness. That's why I like to go to Bombay because there are still people who knew him. Even fifteen years ago if someone came to me with I Am That and asked about earnestness, I would say if he would have said it, he was bullshitting everyone and even Nisargadatta was a bullshitter. But I still liked him. They would say that even Nisargadatta says that. I would say, fuck it even if God says that, it's bullshit. Does the name make it any better? Someone translates something Ramana said and repeats that Ramana said it. I would say in the name of Ramana, kill him.

Kill Ramana and be what-you-are. What-you-are never needs any Ramana as Ramana never needed any Ramana. But if now you make a religion of what he said or not said and you fight about what is true Ramana and what is not true Ramana, it's all a Ramana-banana in that sense. It makes you a banana sitting in a chai-shop and fighting about true Ramana. Then there are all the lineages of 'my true master'. If I try to destroy that, it's not because I don't like it, but because it's a total trap for you. It's like a butcher having all the certificates of tradition – Our butchery is here since two hundred years, believe us we really know what we do. This is the same bullshit of tradition.

Q [Another visitor]: That's a very good example...

K: I always try to make it picturesque so that you can imagine how it is. It's like our cake is the best, our bread is the best because we are doing it since five hundred years. It's like having a wedding anniversary – We are having our fifty years of wedding, I know what is marriage. [Laughter] You just didn't have the courage to leave your wife, that's all. And everyone says, 'Congratulations, I could never do that, I envy you'. There are so many anniversaries, birthdays; it's all like a funeral. Do you really think you did something that you managed fifty years with someone?

Q [Another visitor]: Ramesh Balsekar knew what marriage is about. He said half of the time I do whatever my wife wants me to do and the other half she does what she wants to do... [Laughter]

Q [Another visitor]: To live the outer life in a good way, we pray to get what we want but if you apply that for the inner life, it's a complete failure...

K: We fail in everything. We only take what is given, but we are not worth it, we didn't work for it – outside or inside. It's never because you did something or you are clever. It's pure luck or destiny.

Q [Another visitor]: I get angry and depressed but then I realize it's like a child having his toys taken away. That makes me even more angry and depressed... [Laughter] I have been like a child with stupid toys...

K: Yes, my dear. That's the only time I agree with you. [Laughter] But you are not alone. Everyone has different toys; precious belief systems. Everyone just steals ideas from somewhere. We are thieves the moment we are born. Nothing belongs to you; you steal from everything and everybody. It's all a second-hand treasure. Ali Baba unlimited!

Q: I'm not able to do anything to throw those toys...

K: Why should you? No one wants you to let go of anything. This idea may be good for someone that he has to throw his toys. No. It's the same. Having or not having... no one cares if you have or not.

Q: So that we may lose interest in that idea?

K: Yeah. But still no one cares... Interest came, interest will go and nothing happened. It's like a relationship – it comes when it comes and it goes when it goes. Not a moment before. Try to end a relationship before it's over.

Q [Another visitor]: It's very freeing seeing myself as more and more ignorant...

K: Ignorance is bliss, I tell you. All the masters have said before, ignorance is bliss. Absolutely not knowing what-you-are and what-you-are-not is bliss. The nature of bliss is that you don't know what is bliss. The nature of reality and Self is you don't know what-you-are and what-you-are-not. There's not even a Self for you. What to do? Every moment you know yourself... hell is on! The hell of knowing, the hell of a knower. Then the Noah [knower] wants to build an arc. [Laughing] True English people always have a pain in their brain when I talk to them. If you are a lover of a language, you are in the most painful position here.

Q [Another visitor]: When people translate from one language to another, it's pretty bad...

K: It's all bad. That's why it's called trans-later. The living words are spoken but not transcribed or translated. That's why Jesus always pointed out that only living words are good company but not the written down dead words.

Q [Another visitor]: Ramana walked on the mountain and had a thorn in his foot. He used another thorn to remove the first one. Then he threw them both away...

K: Then they made a teaching out of it. Like a stone in your shoe – you don't keep it. You just walk without it. That's like the 'me'. You don't make it like 'The day I lost my me-day'. That's like making a famous day of your so-called awakening. Then they all remember and write books about it. Every day you lose it so many times but you don't make a fuss about it.

Q [Another visitor]: In the beginning you just sat quiet in Arunachala...

K: No. I spoke as much as I speak now. Actually I was bored in

Bombay listening to psychotherapy questions at Ramesh. Ramesh pointed out that Arunachala was his true influence. So after two days I thought why shouldn't I better go there rather than listening to him.

Q: You sat there for a long time...

K: Ramana sat there for sixty years. I may sit another thirty, I wouldn't mind. You will be bored anyway, that's why you cannot imagine anything like that. Now you have to go to the shaking master, then somewhere else, always expecting something. But the boredom does not go. The whole world is like a shopping mall, trying to get rid of the boredom by buying something. You read for it, you watch television. The tendency is to get rid of this boredom inside.

Q: It seems like people have started feeling constant boredom quite recently...

K: No. Boredom was there since the beginning of time. In England they even have boarding schools. [Laughter]

Q: There is not much mention of boredom in literature, at least not in Shakespeare...

K: Why did he write all those things? Boredom is the master of someone writing all those things. This feeling of emptiness inside, wanting to fill something with something what they think is beauty. Where does all of that come from if there would not be this empty feeling of boredom; the senseless experience trying to make sense in life, trying to fill it up with something what is worth filling it up with.

Q: It may be because beautiful feelings come up...

K: [Laughing] And I tell you they come up from boredom. From the depression where no one is, there arise both the sides – the beauty and the ugliness. That's God in his so called boredom state of awareness. For the phantom who is used to action around him, awareness is more boring. From there arise the oneness and separation. In oneness, there is beauty and in separation, there is ugliness. Both come from the same origin.

Awareness is the sense of rest and it's boredom because you cannot be there as a 'me'. Whoever goes to the rest of awareness, goes to the rest of boredom and from there something arises but it's not because he could avoid it or something. It's just like that was an expression of boredom which is sometimes very beautiful and sometimes very ugly. I meet artists sitting twelve hours a day sitting in front of a white canvas really trying to be bored. Then they get angry and paint something, from there come angry paintings and then they look back and say it's not so bad. Because boredom makes you careless in a way. You are so fed up of everything and then comes inspiration. It's not like hobby artists who paint out of hobby; it's out of a pressure.

Q [Another visitor]: Was Buddha deluded or lying when he introduced the idea of enlightenment?

K: It depends when he talked about it, whether it was before or after the enlightenment experience of his body. It's like the Bible, it is full of what Jesus said about love and harmony and peace. But when Jesus died on the cross and Christ woke up, then he became Shiva, he destroyed all what Jesus had said before. So, it depends when Buddha said that, while he was on the way or when he was the absolute failure. Buddhism was created two hundred years after Buddha died.

Q: So, it's like a poisonous belief system?

K: If you ask me, I would say yes. The idea of enlightenment is a carrot that keeps the donkey running. That's hell, even the idea that you need to be enlightened to be what-you-are is poison. The snake of knowledge bit you and now you think that you have to know yourself to be yourself.

Q: So, when they talk about Buddha getting enlightened under a tree, is that a lie?

K: When you go into it, whatever can be said it's a lie. Whether an enlightened one says something or an unenlightened one says something, both are lies. Even the idea of enlightenment is a lie.

Q: You can say it's like a functioning of a television?

K: Even that is a lie. There was never any television functioning. The energy just showed itself as a television. If at all, it's a functioning of consciousness. The functioning does not depend on a working television. The functioning continues with or without a working television. Even to call something as a television is already a lie. But what else can you do? It's a functioning of ignorance. That's the way ignorance works. And only in ignorance, there's television. What came one day and will be gone one day, can that be real?

Q: It's real in the sense that I can see something now...

K: Is that real? Whether the experiencer is real? Where was the experiencer last night?

Q: He was experiencing something else last night...

K: Where?

Q: I don't know...

K: You imagine that he was still there. And where was this experiencer before you were born? In another hotel? What does this reality depend upon? An idea which is born. An idea that is born now calls something as real or unreal. But the idea that's born is false from the beginning. You can try rebirth techniques and go back to the seed of 'I' back to Adam and Eve but you still cannot find what-you-are. Maybe when you go back, you end up now because this is the seed of all what happens before. The dream is only there because there's a relative dreamer. Talking about Reality is already a joke. Where is your belief system hooked on? It needs a presence of you. But already that presence is a doubtful presence. Out of a doubtful presence you try to create a doubtless Reality.

But that what you create with the doubtful presence of a 'me' will always be a doubtful presence of Reality. It's always a maybe.

Then there's a question, Am I or Am I not? What am I? Who Am I? All of that comes out of a doubtful 'I'. And there will never be any solution to that. That's the presence of consciousness; always doubting itself. Then inquiring into its true nature. It thinks this 'now' cannot be it. When there's a now, there's already a doubt. When there's a now, it asks – What is now? What is that what is now? What is the now of the now? Never ending story because you will never know the nature of the now, as scientists will never know the nature of energy. Scientists cannot explain how electricity functions. They only explain the results, they cannot explain electricity. They now come to the limits of trying to find the nature of things.

Energy cannot be known because if energy can be known, there would be two energies – one energy knowing another energy. The moment there are two, it is relative – one knowing another. So, it will never know itself. That what is energy, that what is life will never know itself. But the moment it knows itself, there are two lives and that will always be relative and doubtful.

Whatever can be known – the knower, the knowing, what can be known are doubtful in nature. But that they can be there, that what-is, has to be as it is. But it will never know itself as That by any relative experience. It is That by being it but not by knowing it. And whatever can be known, will be relative – a dream of relative experiences. A creator, creating, what can be created. It's all relative, a relative God, a relative spirit, a relative man.

But That what realizes itself as the father, the spirit and the son, you can call Heart. But Heart doesn't have any Heart. It will never know Heart. It never knows what-is and what-is-not Heart. But whatever way it realizes itself, it's just a different way of realizing itself, but it's never that what-it-is. Reality can never realize Reality. It can only realize itself in differences. Then there are seven different ways of realizing yourself. The beauty of that is they never make you more or less as you already are. But you will never know yourself in one of them in any relative way – never.

Absolutely you are knowledge. But that you never lost, so you cannot find it in one of them. And now you are looking all over in all the wrong places because wherever you can find something, you will not find what-you-are. You cannot find Reality in the unreal. I call it unreal because whatever you can experience is not real; it's not your nature.

There are many who say that now I take myself as real so whatever I experience must be real. That's why it's so unbelievable that even that is fake. The purest notion of 'I' is already false. The purest notion of awareness, the purest what you can be, is already false. That you cannot imagine. But already that is an imagination of what-you-are. The purest imagination. But even the purest imagination is an imagination. So, there was never anyone who made it. That's the beauty of it that there was never anyone who was enlightened and none of you will ever make it; as no one else before made it.

That's why the diamond sutra says that there was never any Buddha who walked on Earth and Buddha will never show up. You listen to it so many times, but you don't believe it. You still believe that there was a real Buddha and real Jesus walking on Earth. Because if you see that there was never any Jesus, never any Ramana, never any Buddha, never any Nisargadatta who were real, you cannot be real anymore. You only survive because you believe there was a guy before who made it. Without the carrot the donkey would not know what to do anymore.

The biggest thing is this belief system does not need to go away to be what-you-are. That's too much for you. You believe that something has to be different to be what-you-are. And if I tell you, nothing has to come, nothing has to go, nothing has to be different in any whatever way for you to be what-you-are – that kills! That nothing has to be killed, that kills you.

Q [Another visitor]: The people who get enlightened do they come back to themselves?

K: Who came back to whom?

Q: Ramana?

K: Ramana was one of the rare one who said – Ramana never realized anything. Ramana is already part of the realization. How can a part of realization realize Reality? He was a rare one who pointed to that there was never any realized Ramana. Whoever came and told him that you are a realized one, he responded, 'That what you see is not Reality and that what is not real, never needs to see, never needs to realize itself'. There will never be any realized one on earth. And Ramana was a rare one who said that and did not bullshit that I know my true nature.

Q: But are they not just words?

K: No. They are pointers to the impossibility of knowing yourself. You still believe there was one who made it. The nature of *Satguru* is where everyone dies, even the *Satguru* into the unknown of That what-you-are. It does not bring you back to the funeral of a known bullshit; into the cemetery of awakened ones.

Q [Another visitor]: Women are more natural in whatever they do, men are more artificial...

K: From where it starts, the first primitive thing is already artificial enough. All of this is the result of the first primitive artificial realization. It's all artificial. I would not make it more or less, it's just different. Women are differently artificial than men.

Q [Another visitor]: What is the symbolic meaning of the upward pointing triangle of Shiva?

K: Shiva is the triangle pointing upwards and downwards. Both are tendencies, one is the creating tendency and the other is the destroying tendency. If you put them together, it becomes like a star. The feminine and masculine tendencies together. The trident of Shiva is first the light of Shiva and then the male and female tendencies. All three together make the trinity of Shiva. It's the same in Christianity.

Q: And what is the third eye of Shiva?

K: It's the perception of the God or the eye of God perceiving itself through those three ways of experiencing itself.

Q [Another visitor]: Is the knower, the knowing and the known same as the father, the spirit and the son?

K: Yes. [Raising his thumb] Perceiver, [Raising his index finger] perceiving, [Raising his middle finger] what can be perceived. The perceiver would be the father, the perceiving would be the spirit and what can be perceived is the son.

Q: The son is like the manifestation?

K: All three are manifestation of that what-you-are. It starts with the father, spirit and son. It's like Creator, Adam and Eve and then Cain and Abel. Father is already the creator. The second is the creating and third is what can be created. That's the way you realize yourself. That what is the Absolute seeing itself as the seer, seeing what can be seen – the whole scenery of awareness, I Amness and the forms. It's like the Heart [Closing his fist] and the expression of the Heart [Opening his thumb, index and middle fingers]. So what is real? The Heart or the expression of the Heart? [Closing his fist] That would be existence itself expressing itself as the father, spirit and the son. [Opening his thumb, index and middle fingers].

That's why I say – I am one with the father, but I am not the father. I am one with the spirit, but I am not the spirit. I am one with man, but I am not man. I am Heart itself – the Absolute experiencing itself as that trinity. The Absolute father, Absolute spirit, Absolute man. When I am father, I am absolute father. When I am spirit, I am absolute spirit. When I am man, I am absolute man. But I am not the father, I am not the spirit, I am not the man. I am That, what is Heart.

What else can you be? And you are That. In this trinity, you shift from one to the other but in the different ways of experiencing yourself does not make you different. In that sense, you can only experience yourself in artificial experiences. The art you are can never be experienced. In that sense whatever you can sense, the sensor, sensing, what can be sensed are artificial experiences but not what is experiencing itself – from the beginning till the end.

That what-you-are is in-no-sense. That's the meaning of being innocent – in-no-sense. That's your true nature – The absolute virgin. Never ever can anyone fuck that what one is. That virginity cannot be lost. That's why they call 'Virgin Mary' because that's your nature, the black Madonna who never knows itself. That's like giving birth but not having any spot on you. It's like nothing ever happened by giving birth to Jesus. So, she never lost her virginity by giving birth. That's why they make the fairy tale of the Holy Spirit and blah, blah and it was not Joseph.

No! What-you-are never gives birth to anything. Nothing is ever born, so nothing will ever die. How can you lose your virginity?

Q [Another visitor]: Why are all three principles masculine? The father, the spirit and the son...

K: No. The spirit is feminine.

Q: But the other two are masculine...

K: No. Son is not masculine, it's like manifestation. Adam is awareness, the archetype of man like lingam, the light. Then comes Eve, the space. These are two principles, the principle of light and the principle of space. That's masculine and feminine. Out of the principle of masculine and feminine come all the men and women and all differences and polarities. That is mankind. It's not like a masculine son. It means the child of the Holy Spirit and the father.

Everyone has a masculine and a feminine side. So, there are no men or women. Would you call someone a woman just because she does not have a penis? Everyone has a masculine and feminine side in totality. Just because you have a penis you call yourself a man and then you have to live like one. [Laughter] It's all bullshit. You are neither man nor woman. Then they say your hormones tell you what you are. What does that mean? Just because you have a menopause does that make you a woman? Then you define what is a woman. All those are concepts coming from ideas.

January 24, 2013. First Talk
Koh Samui, Thailand

Chapter Two

By Trying To Be The King Of The Kingdom, You Are King Doomed
~

Q: You use the term inquiry differently than everybody else. You say inquiry is simply an aspect of realization of consciousness inquiring into itself...

K: Realization is Self inquiring into itself. The whole realization is inquiry. It's like a pioneer who goes discovering something or doing something – like a scientist. That's every moment. It's not that it's just an aspect of it. The whole realization is inquiry.

Q: That's quite a difference than having a special inquiry...

K: I know, that's the difference. Meditation is a way of Reality realizing itself, it meditates about itself. But without the intention that it knows itself. It's meditation just because it meditates but not with the expectation that it gets something out of it. If there's a conscious inquiry happening, there's no expectation of really finding yourself. But if there's an inquirer, inquiring about the self-inquiry, then it becomes the personal story. That there's something really you can find by inquiry, that you can really find your true nature. Then it becomes a bit ridiculous. That's the main difference.

Q: That's quite a difference from what Ramana or Nisargadatta said...

K: No. They said that consciousness will inquire forever. Consciousness is already an inquiry of the Self into itself. But the Self never expects to find the Self in the inquiry. But you make it your inquiry, that's ownership. That makes it a hell – your expectation. Otherwise it's just a meditation without expectation and without intention.

Suffering or discomfort is only when there's one expecting something by what he does. Then inquiry becomes work. And you work for being paid later. So, you are in business, you are a slave of an idea. That's everybody's normal business.

Q [Another visitor]: So, I must just give up...

K: No. You would make it as a different kind of work again, a different technique. Whatever you do from your position, is trying to get an advantage by doing something or not. You cannot stop it. That's your field. When you understand that all is futile, then you get frustrated and you say 'May be if that doesn't work, I give up everything'. You play a child who is totally disappointed by his doing. Then you say 'Then I don't do anything anymore'. It's like a little child inside who wants to make a revolution. He says if it doesn't work as I like it, I don't want to know anything about it anymore. This little anger beast wakes up.

Q: And when that plays itself out?

K: It will always be there. God as a little child being disappointed by himself. There was such a big promise at first and now it sees it's all empty bullshit. Then you want to fuck it all. This anger of God is quite amazing. He gets angry about himself. The stupidity is unlimited, I tell you. He even wants to kill himself in that. He looks for revenge. He says 'If he doesn't like me and I don't get what I want, I don't want him anymore'. Then suddenly it's a spoiled relationship; now you want a divorce.

It's the same having a relationship with God or someone else, you want to get something. And if he doesn't deliver what you like, you fuck him – I hate him, I don't know him, I want a divorce, there is no God.

Q [Another visitor]: Isn't it possible for the inquiry to happen not in this way...

K: You cannot do relative inquiry differently. It will always be with expectation.

Q: But even knowing that annoyance doesn't change that fact that there's no point in it...

K: You still have to inquire. You can inquire as a little God who expects something from himself, from what he's working and needs a pay day, or you are just that what-you-are enjoying yourself in inquiring, in looking and not finding yourself. That's the joy of not finding yourself in anything – being That what can never get lost. What's the problem? And still you have to look for yourself. This paradox is permanently running everywhere. Even by not having lost yourself, you have to look for yourself. Isn't that fantastic?

And I sit here and tell you, you better enjoy not finding yourself because that's the joy of not finding yourself anywhere. But expecting yourself to find in something, peace or anything – you are fucked! The realization will never stop; I tell you that the next moment will be there. And that is meditation in its nature. Your nature is meditation but there is no place for any meditator who expects something to come out of that meditation. It is a fiction; an imagination of the 'me' and now it became your reality. What a joke!

Q: In the last meditation retreat that I went to, the energy was quite oppressing. It was like trying to beat your mind up that you are not doing it right...

K: Yeah. That you are not right, you are not worth, you are not honest in it, not truthful – all these bullshit questions.

Q: The antithesis to that is seeing this as childish…

K: There is no in-between. When you are what-you-are, no problem. The moment you are not what-you-are with this childish idea, this imagination of the 'me', you are fucked. It's already a punishment from yourself, being not what-you-are. You punish yourself immediately when you are not what-you-are. And it doesn't need anyone else to punish you. You punish yourself very severely. The moment you are not what-you-are, that is punishment already. That's why I always call it the U-punish-ads. [Laughter]

I know that by heart. The moment I am not what I am, it feels complete discomfort, you feel fucked, you feel frustrated, you feel like a little worm of time and existence is pressing you under something, you are never good enough, self-pity immediately jumps in. Poor me, why me? Blah, blah, blah… The whole bullshit of 'me'.

Or you are what-you-are and this carelessness is uncomparable with anything. This peace of carelessness you cannot own. But the 'me' jumps in when you want to stay there. Then you make it some special thing. You immediately make it special and then you are fucked again.

Q: So, there's absolutely no control on when are you in the one or the other?

K: I am never in the one or the other. I just talk about the differences of experiences. But not one of them makes me more or less. Even being in the experience of traveling, I am still what I Am. So, it still doesn't count. This hell of mind-fuck doesn't have to go, this hell comes and goes as everything. There's no problem for what-you-are. If you make the other one as your natural state, then you discriminate again. In both ways, you have to realize yourself; in heaven and in hell. In meditation without meditator; in the impersonal way or in the personal way. Both are always there – heaven and hell wait for you. Just differences but it all makes no difference. That's why I talk about it. If I would make that a better way, meditation without a meditator, it is different to meditation with a meditator. And both are just different experiences; different ways of realizing yourself.

But by feeling little, you don't become little and with the feeling of the absence of the little with the immense peace; doesn't make you That! Both are dreams. That's the nice thing about it – both are dreams. There's no advantage in one and no disadvantage in the other. But if you listen to it, I could make it an advantage. Then you feel more like a worm on the other side.

Q [Another visitor]: It feels like it is an advantage…

K: It is an advantage – but no one has it.

Q: But it still feels like an advantage…

K: That doesn't matter. Only for Russians there are advantages. [Laughter]

Q: But it's a fact…

K: It's not a fact; it's just that you are fucked by that idea. So, many feelings. It's all different but it doesn't make any difference. So, what's the problem?

Q: No problem…

K: There are many problems but no one has them. There is no ownership in anything. Even in the experience of ownership there is no ownership. We can make different states and better states, but your natural state is that you don't even know any natural state. For what-you-are there is not at all any natural state. That's your natural state – by absolutely not knowing what-you-are and what-you-are-not.

But the moment there is knowing; with or without the knower making differences; only in relative one makes differences. For what-you-are, still there is no difference.

Q [Another visitor]: Then the imaginary one must be a ghost that suffers…

K: For sure. Being a ghost is suffering already.

Q: It makes things up which are not there...

K: But that's the nature of the ghost. What can the ghost do? He has to be in the kingdom of ghosts. Then he makes ghost efforts and ghost achievements. That's why it's called a phantom world, where the phantom has to do as the phantom has to do; striving for perfection, striving for getting paid for what he has not done. That is his job. A slave has to behave like a slave. Then he looks for a master but the master is the same slave as the slave. Both are phantoms.

Q: But the phantom is not different?

K: There is a difference but it doesn't make one. Of course there are differences, but they don't make a difference. To say that there's no difference is just another difference.

Q: Does the Reality know anything?

K: Reality knows everything but itself.

Q: And realization happens?

K: Realization never happens. You are fishing now. I tell you there is no fish that you can fish. All the fishes stink, all the concepts that you call about reality, all are stinky fish. All your conclusions, all your understanding, all your precious whatever, it's all fishing – just statements.

Q: It's fishing for getting something...

K: Of course you fish to get something. You sit here to get something. What else can you do?

Q: At the same time speaking just happens...

K: Who says that? Who makes it that this is 'just' and this is 'not just'. Why do you need to pronounce it and justify that it is just an action.

Q: It's just pronouncing...

K: No. You are not just pronouncing. You want to have an advantage out of the understanding. You are a greedy bastard, you know that. God fishing for fish, he becomes a greedy bastard. My control system is just an action, so I can have peace in it. You want to get paid by peace that it's just an understanding; it's just an action, so I can get some rest in it. You get paid immediately. You are a businessman, you know that – Absolute businessman; as everyone.

And I just point to it. I don't make it bad or good. It's just a businessman fishing for being paid. It's like being paid with a little rest, so that you can rest in that understanding. You meditate for business. Everything is for business.

Q: It seems like the business starts as soon as speaking starts...

K: Even before the speaking starts, the business has started already. People are even quiet – for business. They think if I'm quiet, I made it. If I speak I am in danger. So, I better be quiet. When I'm quiet, I get paid more. If I'm a worker and I don't complain, maybe I get my money easier. Always a counter inside, calculating – how can I be better off? Permanently busy, trying to make life bearable. A little understanding to make it a bit more bearable.

Q: But it happens automatically...

K: You don't have to justify it. Just fuck! [Laughter] Let it fuck, you don't have to justify that the fucking comes automatically. Just fuck! Who is interested how it works? Or how you fuck, whether it's a good fuck or a bad fuck. This whole thing is a mind fuck anyway. Otherwise without a lingam penetrating the whole space, there will be no universe at all. The whole universe is a mind-fuck. So, don't be so concerned about the little one inside.

If the whole thing is a mind-fuck – spirit fucking spirit, what about this little one? It's just a side-effect of the absolute mind-fuck of God. But everyone thinks, if I don't fuck inside, God will be pleased with me. God really gives a fuck about your quiet mind. Just to point out that you are absolutely irrelevant for existence – believe it or not. Whatever you understand, whatever you try to justify, no one needs it. No one gives a shit about your little endeavour, and ever and ever.

Q: So, there's absolutely nothing to be gained from trying to renounce your actions?

K: Again you gain a fruitless action there. Then you feel special again that all what you do is just for doing. You will always find a special way of pleasing yourself. [Teasing] Now I am just doing things without expecting something because I saw everything as empty – sounds good. And many teachers are like that. They claim that now they are in pure action and you are now in dirty actions.

Q: Will getting a lobotomy help? When your brain is operated to a moronic state...

K: By minimizing you to the maximum, you are what-you-are. But not by leaving any idea what you can be or any advantage. This is like an implosion into That.

Q: But if you say that whole universe is looking for an advantage, how can I be otherwise?

K: Even you don't have to justify yourself. [Pointing to previous visitor] He tried it already. Poor me! If the whole universe is like that, how can I be different? You place yourself again in this pitiful state. I am always fascinated that the almighty himself puts himself in this pitiful 'me'. It's fantastic! What a divine comedy! The almighty claims that I don't have power. The Absolute knowledge says – Poor me, I don't know. What can I do? I am still fascinated by what I Am.

I can only say, as you are absolute knowledge in whatever experiences, you are absolute stupid. But still your absolute nature is not lost. You are just the absolute knowledge in absolute darkness; and you are absolute stupid in the light. But what can you do? Then you ask me how can that happen that the absolute almighty is in a self-pity. Then I have to say, you cannot miss one little experience of yourself. And all the pitiful things have to be as all the other things as well. You cannot miss one little aspect of your almighty and absolute nature.

Even the most pitiful experience, you cannot miss. And being a seeker is the most pitiful one. Being human, having a mind, what is more pitiful than that? Then the humans think they are the crown of existence. They are fucking ass-holes of existence; trying to become like God. That's the most pitiful circumstance of God; trying to become himself. Then even believing that by being human you are closer to your nature. It's amazing! It's fantastic! The fantastic ride of ignorance.

Q [Another visitor]: In Buddhism they say that only in this human life you can get enlightened...

K: Yeah. It only needs one important fucker to make you another important one. Every religion claims that they are the only way to peace or God or anything. If they tell you that you are human or you are Buddhist or even that you can listen to me, it's important. It makes you very fucking important. [Mocking] That you can even listen to what I say now because I am that. I am very precious incarnation of existence so that you can even listen to me. How many carrots?! How many ways consciousness enslaves consciousness?! Fantastic! The traps are so fantastic and they make you so blind because the traps are made by yourself and you cannot miss one of them. You will always trap into the next shit. [Laughter]

You are the Para-ox and it is all bull-shit. This Ox has no balls but now he claims to have balls. [Laughing] Imagine, God with balls. Then he really has problems; having a ball or two.

Q [Another visitor]: So, in the end it's just a divine accident?

K: I tell you, there's no end. In the beginning it was a divine accident, so you may say that even the end is a divine accident. Even the idea of the beginning is already an accident. You may not find any beginning. Maybe waking up never happened. Maybe reality and realization never started because they are one in nature. Reality never started to realize itself. Absolute silence! Nothing ever happened.

Q: But realization is so tangible...

K: The fragment wants to explain the machine. He only wants to look at the beautiful fragments. Now you need a de-fragmentation.

Q [Another visitor]: I have many different concepts in my mind that Orange is good for me whereas vomiting is another feeling. Now I mix all the concepts together and it feels like orange vomiting...

K: You talk from a reference point of a Shiva and Shiva has a story of likes and dislikes; what feels good and what does not feel good. It's stored in the hard disk; in the brain. That's his-story; it's not a story of what-you-are. It's a his-story of Shiva but not the story of the Self. For what-you-are there is no need of any change. The story of Shiva will continue; in differences, in polarities.

But trying to make both as one is ridiculous. There is only a story of Shiva because of those polarities. Shiva can only continue in polarities; in likes and dislikes. That's the way of this story. Even consciousness has a like and dislike. The presence of consciousness is hell and the absence of consciousness would be heaven. Consciousness already inquires and wants to get rid of consciousness – by meditating, by inquiry.

So, the absence of consciousness is bliss for consciousness. The presence of consciousness is already hell. Because consciousness knowing consciousness is separation. In the absence of consciousness there is not even a consciousness who could know consciousness, that is heaven. Consciousness is swinging between heaven and hell. Presence is hell and absence is heaven. That is orange and vomiting; absence of Shiva is bliss, presence of Shiva is hell. In the little one and in the big one, there are polarities. Every night, no one complains about the absence of Karl or Shiva.

That's why Ramana says it may not be so bad because no one

complains about deep sleep. The absence cannot be so bad. You can only complain in the presence and then it's too late. In the whole day, in the presence, you are longing for the absence at night.

Q: I think rats are more intelligent than we are...

K: I would say cockroaches are better. [Laughter]

Q [Another visitor]: The seeker keeps going up and up in a purgatory, suffering every inch on the way...

K: Mea Culpa! And you are guilty – maximum culpa. You are guilty to the maximum, absolutely guilty for everything.

Q: The whole hierarchy idea in spirituality never appealed to me...

K: But that's the story of human history; it's made out of hierarchy. Why should it stop in the spiritual or any other way? They are trained to make hierarchy. They make it a stairway to heaven not a walkway.

Q: You talk about the tiger playing with the mouse...

K: Just enjoying the play, but never eating the mouse because if the tiger eats the mouse even once, there would be no tiger and no mouse anymore. Even if he tries to eat the mouse, he cannot. You can say consciousness is the mouse and the tiger is the Self. The tiger is never hungry and the mouse always wants to be eaten but the tiger gives a fuck. This tiger has no teeth.

Q: I like the analogy of angels more...

K: But the angel you will meet will be Lucifer – the fallen angel. He will test you or St. Peter, he will wake you and ask – Is there any idea left? Do you still give way to relative beauty? Or beautiful words? Is there someone who owns something? My beauty, my understanding.

This is the eye of the needle. No knower will ever enter the kingdom of Heart. The kingdom of beauty does not allow any idea of beauty. The nakedness you cannot achieve – by whatever you try. All the beautiful words that are in Church is poverty.

Q [Another visitor]: What do they mean by the eye of the needle?

K: Jesus said if you want to join the kingdom of Heart, you have to come as you are. What does that mean? By just being what-you-are, what-you-cannot-not-be, you are already in the kingdom of Heart. But there is no owner of the kingdom of Heart. There cannot be any owner of that Absolute Heart – ever. Never was, never will be. No owner will join anything.

But if you are, what-you-are, you are already in the kingdom. Otherwise, you are king-doomed. By trying to be the king of the kingdom, you are king doomed and that is painful. You must be joking, trying to be the ruler of That. What a joke!

It's fantastic. The moment you control something, rule something, it rules you. The very intention to own, to control, controls you. You can even control the whole universe, but you still will be imprisoned by that. Because if you control the universe, the universe controls you. You are still in the same pitiful position as before. You may have infinite siddhis, infinite control, you may control the entire existence, but you still will be a pitiful bastard. You could know whatever can be known, whatever there is to know. But you still will be a relative knower of a pitiful kind. So, all the avatars, they have no advantage in that position. It's just a different kind of pitiful existence.

But it's so fucking easy just to be That what-you-are. No need for anything, nothing has to come, nothing has to go. How often do I have to repeat that?!

Q [Another visitor]: When drama knows drama, it becomes a melodrama...

K: When Rama knows Rama, it becomes a drama. If Rama knows his wife, it becomes a melodrama. [Laughter] Then it becomes a family business. Shiva and Parvati. There are a hundred-and-eight different names of Parvati.

In India they have a story, God knowing himself was lonesome and from that he created all the imaginary family business. And he cannot just create one wife. The moment he starts to create, he can only create everything; whatever comes with it. He cannot just create a little family around himself. No. The moment he starts to vibrate, trying to create – look what comes out of it! [Laughter] The first existence has the question – Why? Then he becomes the why-brator. [Laughter] Then out of that 'why' explodes the universe.

Then I have to sit here and tell him – Why not? Does it makes you more or less than what-you-are? However it is whatever is the next. Whatever was, did that make you less or more? Whatever is, does that make you less or more? Whatever will be, will it make you less or more? No! None of that makes you more or less as what-you-are. That's the pointer to your very nature who never gets more or less in anything. Knowing more doesn't make you more, knowing less doesn't make you less. So, what about all of that? Counting your little insights, counting your little understandings, counting your little family members and counting what you have and what you don't have. But all what you own, will never make you more and whatever you lost never made you less. Where is the fucking problem?

Q: I couldn't accept that you couldn't contribute anything to existence. But now I'm tired of that idea...

K: For many people bhakti gives blissful moments when they feel they can let go of something; like a little orgasm of how I can let go. But even that confirms a relative ownership. Now by owning less, I become more what-I-Am. This idea is very strong. As more I give I become what-I-Am. The more I give, the more nothing I become. It's another trap of more or less. Suddenly then the idea of less becomes better than the idea of more. Tricks unlimited! The story continues.

Q [Another visitor]: Is surrendering also a trick?

K: Surrendering is another trick. What is yours to surrender?

To what? Who needs to surrender? The answer is always 'me'. Who needs your surrendering? No one. Only a phantom needs to surrender. Then a phantom surrenders – wonderful. Devotion, gratitude, all of that makes you special and that's what you need. A special phantom devoting. Survival is everything for that little one.

So, give up, giving up; devote devotion; renounce renunciation. All what cannot be done. You will fail forever trying to renounce renunciation. But for what-you-are it is the easiest. Every night it gives up you and the renouncer, the devoter, the bhakti and all what can be known or done. In one instant it's gone. And every morning it's stupid enough to pick it up again. But why not?

Q [Another visitor]: The first helplessness is waking up...

K: Yes. The first experience of helplessness is that you cannot avoid waking up. Because if there would be one who could avoid waking up, he is already awake. It's already too late. That what is not there, cannot help it. There is no way. The moment you are, maybe you can avoid waking up but there is already one who is awake. So, it's too late. But the moment no one is there, there is no need.

Q [Another visitor]: There are moments when this comes naturally...

K: That's what you are here for – that the answer comes by itself. Then I can just go home. That's my last hope. That the little Karl in you just gives you the answer; radical answers.

Q: Maybe I am asking the same question again...

K: Of course you do. How can you not ask the very same question again? It's just a variation of 'why'. All the questions are variations of 'why' and all my answers here are the variations of 'why not', you know that. The 'why' comes and I sit here as the 'why not'. Then there are variations of 'why' and variations of 'why not'. There is only one question – Why? And one answer – Why not? You variate in 'why' and think that one day I will find a question which will give me the right answer. Why else do you look for questions? Or do you look for answers and then find questions? What comes first the answer or the question? Can you even question something what you don't even know before? You can only have a question because you know the answer already. It's amazing! How can you otherwise come up with a question?

You have to know what you don't know to ask for that. You do 'as if' you don't know.

Q [Another visitor]: There is a joke that the answer is inside you; but it's wrong... [Laughter]

K: [Laughing] Wrong question, wrong answer.

Q [Another visitor]: When I have moments of joy or sorrow which are not due to the immediate circumstance...

K: You cannot claim that joy was there because of you. Maybe the joy is there when you are not there and then a little bit later you jump in again and the joy is gone.

Q: But they are experienced...

K: No. If there would be reality in it, it should be right here. Where are they now your bloody moments of joy? Even for you it's a hear-say. You tell yourself something. It's an imagination; you try to remember maybe it was something like this, maybe not. Even you don't know how it was. You don't even know if there was a last moment. You imagine that there was a past or future. Then you call it your so-called joyful moments. You don't even know if they exist. It's like a fleeting shadow; like a virtual reality in your computer. Ask your computer if it is real.

Q: A lot of poets have written about these moments...

K: Does quantity of something confirms it to be true?

Q: So, the visions and mystical experiences confirm nothing?

K: They are empty as everything. Now you try to make emptiness more precious than something else. So, emptiness becomes another object which you can experience.

Q: But the mystical experiences show you something...

K: What do they show? What's the difference between a sip of coffee and a bloody spiritual experience?

Q: It is an inferior reality...

K: So, there are two realities? Do we talk about two realities now? Now you make reality relative and you complain that it's all relative and it's not satisfying. You are self-guilty. You will be punished by being in the hell of two realities. [Mocking] My Real-teeths (realities) are gone, now I have the fake one.

I am more wondered by the questions like why is it called appetizer and why not appe-teaser? Anyone has an answer is welcome. [Laughter]

Q: (Rainer) Rilke had this experience of angelic hierarchies. So, the experiences of the higher realms...

K: He was hired by the higher; enslaved by the idea of higher and the higher confirmed him that there is a higher. If you ask me, I would say it's the same ignorance as everything. It's not worse than knowing what is one plus one. Now mathematics tells you one plus one is not always two, it may be three, sometimes five.

Q: When one has a blissful experience, should they just dismiss it as nonsense?

K: They should just take it as the next sip of coffee; if they can. Because that's what it is – just the next. There's nothing special in anything for what-you-are; I tell you. And that one who makes it special is part of the dream, dreaming about hierarchy.

Q [Another visitor]: Does the stairway always go up? It may go down as well...

K: If you see the stairway up, you feel down. If you already imagine to be up, then you are arrogant. Both is bad.

Q: In heaven the river is full of wine...

K: Yeah but you cannot drink it. If all drink from that, there would be no river anymore.

Q: But Krishna has twenty-thousand *gopis*...

K: That's why I say 'go-peace' (*gopis*); let the peace go. Whatever peace can go may go now and just be what-you-are. That's a good position. I wish you a hella-lujah – The hell of a knower; that's the worst.

Q [Another visitor]: If in the vision there is an enigmatic vision that someone is hell. Doesn't that imply an enigmatic element?

K: But who needs for it to make sense? You can answer this question yourself – 'me'. And who is this man who needs special visions?

Q: I don't need them. But if they happen...

K: They are still as bullshit as everything else. You know suffering means you being arrogant and special. This little bigot, this arrogance of God, this born-apart, this little Napoleon scientist inside who always wants to have special experiences that he likes and wants to avoid the experiences he doesn't like. This is the nature of hell because it means that you are the devil 'me' having the idea of speciality and heaven and hell and all of that. Even the idea of God is hell.

Q: It's not because you want to make it special...

K: Why else would you make it as a special event?

Q: It may be no more special than any other event...

K: Then why do you mention it?

Q: Just like we mention any other event...

K: Now you are lying and you will be punished for that lie tonight. But in one way you are right, by trying not to make them special makes you special again. Whatever you do or don't do... [Laughing] What else can you do then trying to be separate and special?

Otherwise you cannot survive as little whatever you are or what you believe to be. How otherwise can you be? Many try to be special then you try to be more special by trying not to be special. This tendency, you cannot get rid of. What can you do?

That's the tendency of every relative God, relative being. He will do everything for survival – even suffer. In fact suffering is welcome because suffering always confirms you. Boredom is very welcome, because in being boring I can survive. That's my last refuge, I take shelter in boredom because in boredom I can be frustrated and in being frustrated, there is one who can be frustrated. All of that is very welcome for that 'me'. What would you do without frustration? What would you do without boredom? What would you do without whatever? All of that you welcome; you take them as a guest who honours you as the one who needs it. It always gives you attention to what you are. Then you swim in the self-pity. What would you do if there would be no pity anymore? You think – Who would I be without pity? So, I better pity myself moment-by-moment.

Q [Another visitor]: I like to think, if I am happy God is happy…

K: Even in the Bible they say if you want to make God happy, just be happy.

Q: But it is different in Hinduism…

K: In essence it's the same. If you are Brahman then Brahman is you; there is no difference. In one of the rickshaws in India it was written, no one remains a virgin, sooner or later life fucks everyone – by showing him how important he was in his story. No way out again.

Q [Another visitor]: If the future has already happened, is there no way of getting slightly ahead of the game? [Laughter]

K: Sorry, no. Stock market was one of my most precious experiences that I could not control. I had an idea of buying a stock but I didn't want to buy it. Then I watch myself going to the computer and watch my finger going down to the 'buy' button. I could not stop it. I knew that I would lose money the moment I would buy. But I could not stop myself buying. The moment you buy it, you cannot sell it immediately because you are interested what will happen next. You are determined to do things even when you know they are totally wrong. No way out!

Q: I intend to put that in a theory...

K: You intend to put theories of preventing discomfort in future. Everyone is trying to do it but no one ever succeeded. Even that you have an experience that you can do something; it was already part of the future. Even that you cannot avoid. That you may have the experience that you are in control. That you could do something. Even that was already meant to be like it, if you like it or not.

Q [Another visitor]: Does intelligence exist except as a concept?

K: No. It's an idea. Intelligence is an idea of intelligence. You can never know what's the chicken and what's the egg. You cannot find where it comes from. Who came up with that idea? It's all chicken. Whatever we can speak about, whatever we can name, whatever... all concepts. The whole universe in its totality is a concept. So, whatever we can talk about can only be unreal. The real can never be known.

But the pointers are that the unreal will always try to know the real – cannot help it. Intelligence always wants to know what is intelligence; always wants to know its nature. No way!

January 26, 2013. First Talk
Koh Samui, Thailand

CHAPTER THREE

The Final Curtain Will Never Fall

Q: I still have a problem with Advaita being separated into what-you-cannot-not-be and the realization. Ranjit (Maharaj) says – forget everything and immediately you are the Self in this very moment. Papaji says – When the mind is quiet you are immediately and totally in That. It seems like they are saying that what-you-cannot-not-be is present here and when the mind is quiet you are immediately and totally in That...

K: No. They don't say that.

Q: How can it be non-dual and there be separation?

K: Your question is how can you be That without a second but still experience yourself in differences? How can That which has no second – not even knowing itself can only experience itself in second.

Q: The non-dual part is...

K: There is only non-duality. There is only one without the second. This is it – in nature; but not as you experience it. Reality and realization are not two. When Reality is resting, there is no Reality. When Reality realizes itself, there is reality in realization. The realizer, realizing what can be realized is not different in nature. There is only life living life in three different ways. But there are still no two in it.

Q: Ranjit says it is possible to experience it immediately...

K: No. It's not immediately; it was never gone. The experience 'you are' or as Nisargadatta would call it – the unpronounced 'I Am' which is your natural state, is always present. But not as an experience of any relative kind. Without the experience 'you are' there is not any experiencing of yourself. So, it's not something that you can attain by being quiet. It never needs to be attained because it was never gone. No mind has to be quiet for that because for that what-you-are, there is no mind – never was, never will be.

Whatever you do is in the realm of dream ideas. And that there can be a realm of dream ideas; you have to be what-you-are. Without your omni pre-sense there can be no experience of presence. So, there's an experience of a presence or an absence of the presence. But even absence can only be because 'you are' and the presence can only be because 'You' are.

Without your omni pre-sense, your omni in-no-sense existence, no experience of existence or non-existence or all what you can experience can be. So, by just being what-you-cannot-not-be you do not attain it. You were, you are and you will be – That. There is no interruption in it. It's not that you become it with a quiet mind. How can that be quiet which was never there? For what-you-are, there is no mind.

Mind means two. But for what-you-are there is not even one. When there's not even one, how can there be two? That's why it's not called 'One without a second' it's instead called 'That without a second'. One is still one too many. Then you make it as if you have to be 'one' to be what-you-are. No. You don't have to be 'one'.

You just have to be what-you-cannot-not-be. And even 'one' is a concept. You don't even have 'to be' – to be! Imagine! That is not in any possibility of imagination. Imagination is only conditioned that you can imagine what you can imagine. It has to be an image. But that what never has an image, you cannot imagine. I don't like what they write in books because you take it wrong anyway. What else can you do?

Q: That was my last attempt... [Laughter]

K: [Laughing] It's a nice promise. I know everyone will be puzzled again and again by whatever is that. But that there can be one who can be puzzled, or not puzzled, he has to be what-he-is. Inspite of being puzzled or not puzzled, you are. Inspite of knowing or not knowing, whatever you can know or not-know, you are.

I like Ramakrishna's basic premise. That even for you to deny to be, you have to be. There is no question: To be or not to be, in that. It's not a question for what-you-are. The final curtain will never fall. The stage is always ready to be played. Every day it opens and every night it closes. There is no final curtain. There is no final understanding. That's why I never bought the idea of final understanding bullshit. You will be stupid again and you will understand again. Why not?

Q [Another visitor]: How does this relate to the statement: The world is illusory; Brahman alone is real; Brahman is the world?

K: Because the nature of illusion is Brahman. In the nature of the world, you cannot find anything other than Brahman because Brahman is the only Reality. So, even ignorance in nature is knowledge or Brahman. So, there's nothing but Brahman or Self; call it whatever. And yet 'you are'. And to that, there is no alternative, no way out of being it. And that's the easiest. That's your very nature that doesn't need any effort to be it. It's an effortlessness of being That. For whatever you have to make an effort, for sure, is unreal. Whatever needs attention, is unreal. Whatever needs anything is unreal.

Q [Another visitor]: You call meditation and trying to control your mind as fascism...

K: It's all fascism. Trying to control something, is what?

Q: Then the mind thinks that it should just lie and pick your nose...

K: Try it. [Laughter]

Q: But...

K: You may try now. [Laughter] If you really succeed in it, I will come to Australia. [Laughter] You cannot leave your finger out of your nose.

Q: But it does away with everything. It does away with the whole system of values...

K: But you still have to worry about your daughters. There's no contradiction in it. Things will happen according to what the future demands for what needs to happen. It's not you who can decide now that nothing can be done and now you can lie down and do nothing. Ha, ha, ha!

Your stomach will be hungry and your bladder will lead you to the toilet and then you have to pee. Things happen by themselves, as they already happen. So, don't worry. No one ever became lazy by that. But That what is your nature is laziness itself; it never did anything. But the dream continues. And it does not even run out of steam. There is an idea that the mind runs for a while and then it rests by itself. Even that is a bullshit idea. As if it's dynamic and when you do not feed it, then the mind gets slower and slower and it rests by itself. Ha, ha, ha!

For who? For whom does the mind stop? It's still a fake mind that has stopped. It may or may not happen. But who cares if it stops or doesn't stop? It needs one who cares. And still there's a little hope that if I don't give any attention to that, if I don't give it energy then it may stop one day. You are so fascinated looking at the fucking mind which sometimes even fakes to have stopped. Then it comes back – (Mind says) It was just a joke my dear, I was just joking. Just having fun. It's like a man who thinks now I have a quiet dick. It will never come up again... Ha, ha, ha! That's why I like the 'Samsara' movie so much. For three years, three months, three weeks, three days the whole body was closed. Then the very first night it wakes him up. The rising of the lost...

I like the word his-story. It's the story of the body, the story of the world. But it is 'his' story and the story will never end. It will always be different but what can you do with it? You will fail and fail and fail to try to stop it. The hamster will always try to get out of the wheel. Consciousness always inquires and tries to find a way out of ignorance.

But that's the joke. Knowledge wants to get out of ignorance but the nature of ignorance is knowledge. So, knowledge wants to leave knowledge. [Laughing] It's always a joke. What to do? But why not? Try harder! So, my dear hamsters. Then the master says one day I will sit on my wheel and nothing will happen anymore. [Laughter] Where is all the fun? I will be fat and lazy, hanging around. Then I need to go to the doctor for sucking out the fat because I don't move anymore.

Q [Another visitor]: But the way out is to see it as a story?

K: No. It's a permanent story of consciousness trying to find a way out of existence.

Q: And the only way out is to see...

K: There is no way out! Even that is not a way out. Now another teddy bear wakes up. She claimed that there is no teddy bear anymore but it just woke up from the winter sleep. [Laughter] The teddy bear said, I thought it was winter but it seems warm here. Why did she put me to sleep? I want to have some fun, the sleep is over. There is not even a 'no way out'.

Neti-neti would mean there is neither a way out nor a no-way out. There are many ways out but by none of the way out, anyone gets out. But there are many who claim that they found a way out. So, there are many exits through which people went out and now they claim they are out and you can get out too. Just move your ass, sit down and meditate. [Laughter] That would be like the inner direction; picking your nose forever. But that's a habit. What to do with the little rabbit inside? It always jumps out and tries to catch the carrot.

Q [Another visitor]: I read that once you had an experience where your body was emitting real light that you could read a book from it...

K: That is a fundamental question. What is 'real' light? Two people looking at the lamp and agreeing that the lamp is on. Would you call that real light? Do you mean if I have a girl friend next to me, she would also be able to read the same book?

Q: Yes... [Laughter]

K: I think you would not be interested in the same book.

[Background noise of chainsaw]

Did you hear the noise before I heard the noise?

Q: I hear the same noise...

K: You hear it now when we talk about it. But before that? Ask someone around here if they all heard it at the same time or only when you give attention to it. Now as everyone gives more and more attention, it gets louder and louder.

No. Light cannot be experienced at all. How can you experience light? What's your idea of light?

Q: It is something that wakes me up and because of which I can see everything...

K: Something that wakes you up?

Q: No. It is a possibility of seeing everything...

K: That's not light. Those are dream reflections on canvas of your perception. Light cannot be seen, come on. Ask any scientist if light can be experienced or can you only experience reflections of light in your eye. Light is not what you can experience, you can only experience reflections of it. Everyone has a different way of experiencing it, like a cat sees it different than you. It can even see at night. Where is the light for you at night? You have your definition of light but then comes the bat that has a total different experience of perception. Even the bat would say that is an experience of light.

Q [Another visitor]: Where does the light in the dream come from?

K: It's same like here. You cannot experience light here. This is the same dream as the night dream, a day dream. But you cannot say what is real here or what is real light or what is real energy. It's only an agreement to call something light because you agreed to something what is dark. Then from your reference point you call something as 'light' and something else as 'darkness'. You can never accept that darkness is as much light as what you call light.

So, it's already a concept of your experience; of your conditioning. Ask a baby what is light? Ask the baby next to that baby if it sees the same. All the second-hand conditioning and concepts which are put in this field and then you repeat something what someone told you. Now you see the world as the world is told to you. Without having a name for the world, without having a name for a tree, what you don't give a name, you don't see.

It's like you have a book in Mongolian and you don't even see the letters, you don't see any sentences. Then after one or two years, you learn to read Mongolian and suddenly there is a totally different thing there. Suddenly there is a story and a whole world opens up for you. But before you can read it, there is nothing. There are only some black marks on the paper.

As a baby there is just light, the light of awareness. Nothing but light, the golden presence of light. Then comes the golden tit and you suck golden light from the golden light of a golden liquid. Then you lose it moment-by-moment because it becomes more like a matter; because people tell you what it is.

Sometimes I think I should not talk about it. But now it's written down somewhere and people remember so it's too late anyway.

Q [Another visitor]: So you are saying, that we can only experience the reflections of light?

K: Yes. Like you can only experience the reflections of a diamond but not the nature of the diamond. It's like you cannot experience energy, you can only experience the reactions of energy. The action can never be experienced; you can only experience the reactions of it. Your nature can never be experienced, you can only experience reflections or aspects in the mirror of awareness but never as you are.

And I sit here and tell you be happy about it. If you could experience what-you-are, there would be two. What you are looking for is hell. If it could really happen that you could know yourself, there would be two selves. I sit here and tell you be happy that you don't know yourself and will never know yourself in anything. You cannot sense yourself and if you could sense yourself, you would be a relative sensor and you could only sense relative sensations. Already that you believe to be a relative sensor sensing relative sensations, you are in the relative hell of being different from something else. That's the whole misery you are in. You believe that you, as a seer, are different from what you see. It's a belief system that was put on to you by your ancestors. It's a tradition of making you stupid – by yourself. And if you find the origin of it, you are the origin of making yourself ignorant.

Falling in love with an idea is the most common root of the ignorance, the root of suffering – love. The only energy that can get you out of absolute into the relative is love. Nothing else can make you so stupid as to leave what-you-are. Your so-called precious love is the biggest trap ever which is built by what-you-are; being the lover and then being different from your beloved. Then even trying to unify yourself with the beloved coming out of a false belief that there is a lover and a beloved. Then they tempt to unify yourself with what-you-are. What a perfect trap! You are the most mischievous bastard you are!

In India they call life a bitch; sooner or later it will bite you. You can play with it for a while but it will bite you because you will suffer about it by experiencing it. You have to pay your price; for your little relative being; experiencing the love for yourself; creating a hell – Hell-a-lujah!

Q [Another visitor]: What a punishment!

K: How many times did I say, the moment you are not what-you-are, you already punish yourself by not being what-you-are. You don't need any other – whatever – to punish you. Just by you not being what-you-are, you are already punished by missing yourself. That's the nature of 'me' – me-sing (missing) itself. And by me-sing itself, it's a song of a 'me' missing and longing – poor me! There the self-pity God starts. God knowing himself and then missing his nature. This miserable bastard! Now there are seven billion missing Gods – and it doesn't matter! He cannot stop it. That's his way of realizing itself. Isn't that fantastic?!

Not even God – the almighty bastard – can stop it. He tries permanently but he cannot. He is absolutely impotent in trying to stop his own realization and change it. Fantastic!

Q [Another visitor]: Once doership is no longer there, isn't there seamlessness between the experiencer and the experienced?

K: Temporary. Every night there is no doership; not even an idea of 'you' and every morning you are stupid enough to pick it up again.

Q: But in the night there is no experiencer and no experience...

K: Now you want to make it a relative achievement again; shifting to better places. There must be better homes than this one; there must be better rooms in this house of God than this relative 'lounge lizard' business here; hanging around the television. That must not be all; there must be some better places. I have to work in this 'first' (state of consciousness) room. I have to read, my entire library is in that room. I want to get rid of everything; I want to go to that empty room where not even a word can be spoken as there is no speaker.

Q: The other day I was watching and saw there was no difference between the experiencer and the experience...

K: Because there was a moment of acceptance and tolerance and that acceptance is like an orgasmic absence of judgment. Then you feel quite well in it. You feel as if you are one with the scenery because there is no resistance or an attempt to avoid it.

Q: But that's temporary?

K: Look at it. [Laughter] What's now?

Q: But can you train yourself in that?

K: Try harder. You tried the whole life to train yourself into it. You want more acceptance and want to have a higher tolerance limit and try to accept everything. Then there are teachers who claim that they did it. [Mocking] If you just stay in the 'now' there is acceptance. You just have to stay in the now because in the now there is no judgment of past and judgment of the future because there is no 'one' who can judge in the now. So, the now would be without a judge. Then they make it a more favorite place – the absence of the one who judges and when there's no one who judges there's no difference. There's an experience of oneness.

If that is your goal, there are many techniques. I think you can even achieve it by going to the red light district in Thailand. If it has to happen, it will happen inspite of your effort. It just happens, by the way. Fantastic! Then it takes you out again. It was just a temporary holiday of the 'me' and then the 'me' comes back. Then he makes a story out of it – of when he was not there.

Q: So you just accept whatever comes up?

K: I don't say anything. If you ask me, your very nature is acceptance, which never needs to accept anything because it doesn't even know what is acceptance and what is not. But the moment you know what is acceptance, you are in trouble. Then you make a difference between accepting and non-accepting; oneness and twoness.

I read in books that many people came to Ramana and asked him – What about oneness? And Ramana said – When there is oneness, there is twoness. There is still one-too-many who is in that oneness. Then Papaji says, where you can land, you have to depart again – if you like it or not. You are already in the departure lounge; even if you have just arrived. You cannot stay for good, anyway. You will always shift between differences of heavens and hells. And you have to be what-you-are in spite of whatever way you experience yourself. If you need a special way of experiencing yourself, that's the nature of a relative 'me' and that's the way devil works. Because in differences, it is the master of time – this devil 'me'. Time means there are two different ways and one is better than the other. That's diabolic. That's the way this master rules.

Q [Another visitor]: I don't like that there's no way out...

K: There is but there is not. You can experience a way out and can even experience to be out. But that one who is out, the moment it is out, it goes back. Because when you really would be out, you would feel so fucking alone and unbearable – without a second – the phantom immediately goes back where there may be suffering.

Q: Is it only the phantom that goes out?

K: Only the phantom can go out. Do you think the existence needs to get out of existence? To be what-you-are, there was never any in and out. It doesn't even know in and out. There's an absolute which never knew any in and outside and never needed anything. But it is not something new. It's not that you enter something or attain it again. It's not a way out; it's just being what-you-are. Nothing has to happen for that. You cannot catch that, you cannot own it.

That's the main thing; you cannot own yourself in any relative way. You have to be the Absolute owner not owning anything and there's no in-between. When you are what-you-are, how can you suffer about what-you-are? For suffering, it needs two. But in what-you-are, there's not even one. And without a one, there's not even a possibility of two.

But the moment you are 'one', you will create two – the second. What to do what is not already done? Wherever it leads you to, will always be a temporary phase just before the next. Empty drama. No one asked you to like it. I am absolutely pleased that I don't have to please anyone – not even myself. That's pleasure itself. The nature of pleasure is to be what-you-are which never has to please or be pleased by anything or anyone to be what-it-is. That's the nature of joy or pleasure or beauty because it never needs beauty, it never needs peace, it never needs anything, just by being what-it-is. That's the nature of satisfaction itself. But in that, there's no one who is satisfied or not satisfied. All the ideas of being satisfied or not satisfied are in the dream; but not in reality. In the dream all of that is there, but...

The judge always has to be justified. He always has to fight, even to exist he has to fight. And his best war is against suffering. He knows as long as I fight against suffering, I can survive as a sufferer. It's like, I want to be healthy. The moment you want to be healthy, you must be sick. So, the sicker, the seeker, confirms himself – just by wanting to be healthy. That's hell. And only in hell you can survive as a devil. So, the devil will make sure that there's hell and many religions are only for that.

God never created any religion, only the devil creates whatever can be created. God never has any soldiers; it never needs any soldiers to fight for him, only the devil needs soldiers who fight for him.

Q [Another visitor]: What kind of God would need to be worshipped?

K: Only the devil needs to be worshipped. Only relative God needs worshipers, believers. What kind of truth needs to be fought for? Only a relative truth, only relative ideas need soldiers who fight for it; or monks or nuns for the maintenance of the business. Only the devil has a business. God has no business.

But you can say even that is a way of God realizing himself; being busy with himself but he cannot stop it – not because he wants it or needs it. That's why it's just for fun. It's an entertainment show of God. And part of the entertainment is all the angels and devils, all the different characters. Indians are much more free in it. There are thousands of Gods and they don't mind because they see all as reflections of Brahman. Brahman is the origin and it plays infinite roles; even if every person is a reflection of it, then why not many Gods? It's just different characters played by consciousness.

Q [Another visitor]: I go to a large Church and it's great, I like God and the church with a big band...

K: Isn't it a fantastic show? The big cathedral and all the music. It's fun, like Hollywood; nothing wrong with it – or right. That's the beauty it's never wrong or right. It's just fun. If you really think it's something really good, then it goes wrong. If you just go for fun, like a bar or beach; just entertainment.

So, I don't say there's something wrong with it. It's just part of the fun. But the one who sits there believes that he's working for God and sitting here is better than sitting somewhere else. Then you are in trouble. Even in ashrams in India people go to masters to sit in their presence and feel very special and blessed that moment. Then there's an arrogance running inside because they are the blessed ones – the chosen ones. Because only God makes them look for the truth, the rest are just masses – pigs and cows and human rubbish. Then you will be punished again. When you are special, you get special attention. [Laughter]

The chosen ones always get a special attention from everyone. You sit there and say I am the chosen one. Then everyone argues on why you are not. You get special attention.

Q [Another visitor]: It's a negative attention…

K: What's a positive attention? The good thing is no one can decide what he decides. If consciousness wants it, it will happen. It's like Hitler believed that as long as he has the spear of destiny, he would win every war; until he lost. So many rumors. Everything is a rumor in that sense because nothing can be proven and no one needs proof. They even took Lamas from Tibet because they wanted to do a dream magic to leaders of the world, just to give them bad dreams. There are so many levels and things that can happen and did happen in consciousness. It's not just the things that are as described in history books which you can read and say it's true because it was written somewhere. History is written by winners and not by losers. In the normal books, these are not written because normal people would just reject it. All the politics is like mafia anyway. Even fascism is creating cluster of same interest to make something work.

But that's religion too. You have a same interest and then you fight for your religion. And I say even the esoteric things are fascism because they gather for the better of the world. I have to say, it's fascism. It's not negative; it's just the way it happens. That's why I call Eckhart Tolle a fascist because he wants to gather his soldiers for the new earth. People of same interest trying to get together to change the world because one alone cannot do it anyway.

Q [Another visitor]: Perhaps this word comes from the word 'fascia'; group of tissues that hold muscles in the body…

K: Yeah, could be the same root.

Q: Without that we wouldn't even be here…

K: Yeah. This fascistic body of cells has to work together otherwise it dies. It's like a nation or a family. So, I say everything is fascism because without fascism nothing will survive. Then people get shocked. It's like an anti-fascistic movie maker in Berlin wanted to kill me. He was so offended when I said everything is fascism, he told me, 'Shut up, you cannot say that'. That's fascism – trying to tell me what I can say and what I cannot.

Q [Another visitor]: Do you think black magic is real in the relative reality?

K: Look here, this is black magic. There are so many witches and sorcerers sitting here. The daily magic is fantastic. The wife cooking a good meal for her husband trying to charm him. It's all trying to charm someone; in whatever way; one level or another. Charming means controlling. Everyone wants to charm. Even when someone puts on a make up in the morning; it's trying to charm. That's the magic of the lady. Or a man dressing differently or going to the gym and making muscles trying to charm someone. Having a nice car is charming.

It's all magic! The whole daily life is magic and charming and trying to control by different recipes of making the other one do as you want. This is the basis of daily life magic. Then, for sure, there are other levels. But you can experience it right now, everywhere. It's very obvious; you see it normally as people trying to control people. But this is charming. All have their techniques and recipes of how to do it. A witch making a soup for the husband who is coming home.

Q [Another visitor]: We do that to our kids as well...

K: Every mother is a witch for sure. [Laughter] Teaching them the defense system of how to survive, what to say and what not to say in life. Everything is magic. The whole world is like a training camp. Then if it doesn't work anymore, you start war; that's different kind of magic.

Q [Another visitor]: In Macbeth, Shakespeare spoke on witches...

K: When you are what-you-are, you are the absolute magician. Everything is magic in that moment. When you have a little insight like Shakespeare, you see that it's all part of life trying to charm life. The snake always tries to charm the snake. It's always a paradise here now; here the snake tries to charm Adam. The paradise business didn't stop, it's here now. Eve is here, Adam is here, the snake is here, the tree of life is here, the tree of knowledge is here. It was not in a different plane, it's here now. The whole story is being played here now.

And you cannot decide where your attention goes in any moment. If it goes to the tree of life, then you are in the oneness. When your attention goes to the tree of knowledge, you are fucked by trying to know yourself. Then you are mind-fucking. I just tell you how it works, but you cannot decide where your attention goes next. It's all available. The Eve is here; the pure oneness space. The crazy wisdom is here. All the different things are here now.

But you cannot decide where your attention goes next because attention has no ruler. There is no ruler who can control attention – never could. God cannot control perception itself because there is no perceiver; no controller in it. It just has to experience himself as whatever. And all the different levels of magic; this paradise business is still running moment-by-moment. But being Adam already is a relative experience. Being Awareness, you cannot avoid. The archetype of man – Adam. Then comes Eve – life. Then come Cain and Able. Sometimes you have to play Cain, then you do things that please God because you want to please existence. But again, praying to God is trying to charm him. Now I do as you want me to do. Can I charm you with that?

Q: What about entities like demons?

K: Look around.

Q: I had a lot of problems with these things...

K: I had so many stories of so-called spirits that didn't know that they are dead – like here. [Laughter] In early nineties we went to a cave where we looked around. There was a bed and table and the last page of the Tibetan book of the dead. We went home and the next day a lady started yelling that she had so much energy and I am not able to get rid of it. I said, look you picked something up. Then we went into energetic things and the thing went out. The next day another friend started yelling. Then they found out that a guy died four weeks ago in a motor cycle accident on the road with instant death. It seems like he didn't know that he died. There was no experience of dying. So, he was still around and she picked it up. So, we said let's put this guy away by going into the absence and showed him how to die. Then it was gone. So, things like this can happen. I like these stories.

Q [Another visitor]: Sometimes people say that some people walk into their bodies…

K: That's why the Church performs exorcism and the Pope opened the department once again.

Q [Another visitor]: I tried Ayuwaska with the intention of purifying myself. But I saw some entities…

K: But with the intention of purification, you open yourself for that and then they come. Maybe they created the church of Ayuwaska for that. Even John of God, the healer claims that there are entities that heal and not him. I like all the stories. It's like a soap opera of consciousness.

In that way, I have nothing against all the stories. If you see people sitting here right now, it's the same ghost story. There's nothing different. If you believe that there are people here or the world is here, it is not any different than believing in entities in a different dimension. And things can happen, everywhere. You can be haunted and everyone puts a spell on you. You promise to make someone happy – like marriage. Everyone has to say yes to it, make a spell. Then the Church wants you to repeat – Are you here out of your freewill? That is why it is called go-spell (gospel). The gospel of Jacob, the gospel of anyone is like charm the world with your words; go and spell the words of God and make them know that there is God.

Q: But when the intention is really good…

K: It's always good intention. Everyone has a good intention from his position because everyone has a reference point that he knows better than existence what is good. And from his side, it is always good intention; as if you know what is good intention. From the other side, you may say it may be dark. But from your side it is good intention. So, it needs two fascists. Mephistopheles in Goethe's Faust always wants to do wrong but the outcome is always good.

Q: The spirit which is evil, forever tries to be evil...

K: And what comes out of it is pure goodness. Even if you try to be bad you cannot be bad because the intention is good from the beginning. Goodness is the nature of God and out of goodness only goodness can arise. How can out of the absolute goodness can anything that is bad arise? Out of peace only peace can arise. Peace realizing itself; there is only the dance of peace – even in the nature of war. Peace can only create peace as good can only create good. Even if you want to have a bad intention, you cannot have one. You can try to be bad but you will never be bad. Maybe if you try to be good, you become bad. But even then you are not bad.

You ask me how I see things. There is only that what is Brahman and in the nature of Brahman there is no second Brahman. It is that what is the nature of goodness and Brahman realizing itself can only realize itself as goodness. Oh my goodness!

Q: But Brahman is prior to all this...

K: It is not prior. You make him special again. He is this all. This is a realization of goodness. Oh my goodness! What else is here? There is only Brahman. The Reality is Brahman and the unreal is the idea that there is good and bad. But even the idea of good and bad in nature is good. So, even the nature of bad is good. It's like the nature of ignorance is knowledge, as the nature of knowledge is knowledge. There is no difference in nature. So, the nature of badness is goodness, as the nature of goodness is goodness.

If you really have a rational, logical, intelligence running you will say yes otherwise you just try to stay in your little devilish stand point of good intention, of having a romantic idea of goodness. Then you don't follow any logic. You only follow what you like to be.

Q: Dr. Pangloss says in this best of all possible worlds, everything happens out of absolute necessity, and that everything happens for the best...

K: I agree.

Q: Voltaire made a joke out of it...

K: Voltaire was a joke.

Q: When you are in the midst of the experience...

K: Who is in the mist (midst) of the experience? That's why it's called the mist of the experience. In the mist; being blinded by ideas. Tell me anything what is bad.

Q [Another visitor]: Can you say torture comes out of a good intention?

K: Of course. The torturer has the good intention to find out the truth. But the result of the good intention may not be so nice for someone. You can say that from your reference point it does not feel so good.

Q: What about the sadist who tortures for their own pleasure?

K: There is no such thing as torturing for the sake of torturing. Then it is not torture.

Q: What is it then?

K: You cannot find anyone because in that there is no one who has a reason for it. It's like me sitting here – that's torture. [Laughter] I mean it. But it's out of a good intention. I feel tortured by the good intention of so-called seekers who want to know themselves. What can I do? It's torture, even to wake up. From the beginning.

Q: I am talking about deliberate torture...

K: There is no deliberate torture. Who can decide to torture? Who can make the decision? You can say that the circumstance dictated one to torture someone. But you cannot find anyone who did that out of his freewill. Now you believe in freewill again. You go back to the Stone Age belief system of free will. Without a free will, there is not even intention. It's just a dance of energy, dancing with goodness. But if you make it free-willy again; as if God's willy can decide what he wants.

But without that you would not have any basis for your concepts. Only because you believe in free will – that is the basis of all what comes later which is good and bad. Without freewill where is your good and bad intention?

Q [Another visitor]: Supposing...

K: Composing – now you want to compose your point for whatever, not supposing.

Q: And you are not composing?

K: I don't know. I just play music. For me, musicians cannot learn to play. Music plays itself and music has no standard of good or bad music. But the moment you have an idea of good music, you are fucked by the idea of good music. Then you have to exercise and rehearse. It needs one who has an idea of good and bad and the basis of that is freewill; that you can decide what is good taste and bad taste. Then you are already in the drama of fighting for your so-called stand point and reference point.

Now we can compose; it is compost putting things together and trying to make it a good composition. So what is it that you are supposing?

Q: I was thinking about some unpleasant experiences that happened to the person whom I recommended a person with good intention...

K: Like your mother giving birth to you. It starts with that, that's the beginning of your drama, your torture, having a body, that there is even one who could be tortured. The potential victim is born out of a mother.

Q: In this case it affects the person's energetic body and not physical body...

K: What is not energetic? The moment you are a separate entity believing in your freewill, you believe in other entities that have freewill. Then you go in the drama of good and bad intention. Then you build an armour around yourself; your defence system runs wild. Then you think that you have to open up but when you are open, your emotional body gets attacked. Then you want to close again. Then you say, [whining] what shall I do? Be open or close? [Laughter] When I am open, I cannot take it and when I am close, I can take a little bit. But I don't feel so good because I am so closed. I don't get what I want because I am so closed. But when I am open sometimes I get what I want but other times it's too much for me. So, I close again.

Then the teachers tell you that you have to open your heart. But when you have an open heart, everyone abuses you because not everyone around you has an open heart. Then you feel that the intentions are not so nice sometimes. With open heart, I go to bed with everyone because I cannot say no anymore. But if I go to bed with everyone, I feel like a prostitute. I don't take money but still I feel like a prostitute. [Laughter]

You have to imagine what the consequences of the open heart mean. It means you have no discrimination anymore between man or woman or anything. You are just open to everything. You make no decision anymore. Everyone wants to have an open heart but then still wants to decide what comes in. It doesn't work this way. Then you want to charm others with your open heart – look at me.

Last year we had a lady who said she had an open heart and she healed herself with an open heart. She became a missionary of open heart. And if you don't believe me, I don't like you. [Laughter] She said, but Eckhart Tolle and Tony Parsons like what I said. I said, but not me. Fuck your bloody open heart, I don't need it. She was really angry. I really like that; an angry open heart! That was fun. [Laugher]

Q [Another visitor]: A bleeding heart...

K: My heart bleeds for you; I have so much compassion for you. Keep your bloody compassion for yourself. Give it to yourself if you need it but not to me. Yuck, I don't need this compassion from someone. It's like slimy bastards want to slime me in with their open heart business. Sleazy, slimy bastards; trying to suck you in their system of open hearts. So, I show them that even that has underlying trying to charm and control someone. And then they say if you don't believe my open heart, you are not so nice.

But if even that is good intention, what to do?

Q [Another visitor]: What is an open heart?

K: What would you say? No discrimination anymore, embracing everything, accepting what-is. As I said, if you really have an open heart with no discrimination and if someone wants to fuck you, you have to go with him. You have to obey to existence. You have to accept the demand of whatever is around you. There is a story of a sage with an open heart. A lady has a baby but she cannot accept it in society. So she falsely accuses the sage as it was his baby and asks him to take care. The sage says yes to everything. Then for ten years he takes care of the baby and the woman comes and asks for taking her son back. He just says yes, take it. That's like open heart, always yes to everything.

Whoever claims to have an open heart, for sure you can doubt. You have to doubt it immediately. The scriptures say the nature of the open heart is the heart that does not know any heart. And doesn't even know what is open and what is closed. An absolute open heart is a heart without an owner. There is no ownership in it. Heart just being heart. But that heart would never claim to be an open heart. And whoever claims to have an open heart is sometimes more closed than the other ones.

Q: What does it mean when you say, I know you by heart?

K: Being what is here [Pointing to himself] and there [Pointing to visitors], I know you by heart. The nature here is not different to the nature there. So, I know you by heart but not by anything else. The rest I am not interested in. Just by knowing me as – That what I am, I know you by heart. Being the nature that is no different here than there, I know you by heart but not by any smell.

Q [Another visitor]: Is that absolute or relative knowledge?

K: That is absolute knowledge – just by being what-you-cannot-not-be which is That what-is, you know everything but you know nothing. And that's the absence of a knower and what can be known in that knowledge. So, by heart I know what I am, but not by any idea, not by any imaginary – whatever. So, this heart has no attributes. When you call it open heart, you make it relative again. That what is an open heart, still has an idea of being closed.

Q [Another visitor]: Perhaps the arrogance unavoidable...

K: I would say the same. Not maybe, it is unavoidable.

Q: Even when I say, 'This is rubbish, that is rubbish' is arrogance...

K: Yeah. Both are arrogance. From wherever you speak, there is a stand point, a reference point. And every reference point is a relative one; it's an arrogant reference point. But every reference point is an arrogant reference point which is different to some other reference point. And arrogance reference point means being apart; being different to something else you cannot avoid. Because every stand point needs a reference point to speak from. What to do? And everyone just has a different reference point and they are all arrogant because for sure, they are not right. You can only speak from a fake one. Truth will never speak anything.

For every concept you pronounce, you need a reference point which is already false. Then a false reference point produces false. So, arrogance is the nature of ignorance; both come together. Every reference point is a point of ignorance. That what is knowledge has no point. It would never speak from one or the other point because there is no difference in knowledge or in truth.

Whatever you can say is ignorance and ignorance needs arrogance. That's the way it is. Even by trying not to do it, you make a different stand point that is arrogance again. Even the one, who claims that I am not arrogant in that sense, is the most arrogant.

Q: It's best to stay silent...

K: That's another arrogance point. Whatever you come up with is another reference point. It's all 'may' or 'may not'.

Q: Is that because I want to own something that's better?

K: If you think you can do something better or make something better, it's very arrogant because then you have to see something what is bad which you can make better. So, in your point of view something is bad and you want to make it better. That's the little Hitler inside; this esoteric bastard that everyone wakes up with called 'me', who always knows better how it has to be.

God becomes like that. The moment God knows God, he knows what is good for God; and what is bad. Then he is even jealous about his true nature – imagine! God gets jealous about God. The God who knows God gets jealous about the God who doesn't know God. Then he even wants to kill himself. So, he is seeking himself not to embrace himself. Actually God seeks God to kill him – moment-by-moment. But he could not find him and yet he is still looking for him.

So, God inquiring into God, looking for God is not out of love. He claims that he loves him to make him come out of his hidden place. I love you, where are you? Come out. But if he would come out, he would shoot him right away. He wants to charm – please come to me.

But even I ask you to shoot whatever comes out; shoot it right away. Whatever duck pops up, whatever concept pops up, whatever idea pops up, just shoot it – out of fun. So, if God pops up, shoot him. If the devil pops up, shoot him. If any concept pops up, just shoot. Don't stop shooting. You are the absolute hunter and you shoot and you shoot and you shoot. In German *schutt* means rubbish.

Just see that even the seer is empty; empty seer, empty seeing, empty what can be seen. Empty, empty, empty. Empty in the sense that it will never make God come out of its true nature. No one can ever charm God to show himself. And no one will ever charm Buddha to show Buddha. So, if you meet Buddha on the way; kill him or shoot him.

Q [Another visitor]: So, the concept of shooting is okay if it's fun?

K: For fun is always okay.

Q: But if you take it as a sadhana?

K: Then it's a criminal act against yourself. Meditate because you cannot otherwise not meditate. Every morning you wake up and meditation is there. But the moment you expect something to come out of that, then it's a crime against your nature. Crime means that you become one who needs something to be changed to be what-one-is. That's the crime against your nature.

Whatever doing that comes out of your doership – of an idea that you can do something to become what-you-are – makes you depending on your doing. So, you become someone who could be attained by action. And just by being an object of time, you suffer. You killed your true nature by trying to make it alive or to see it or to make it exist. That's the criminal act; you become a murderer of yourself. You kill yourself the moment you know yourself.

But what to do? Your love for yourself is always so strong that you would rather kill yourself then not trying to know yourself. That's why when Moses came down and they made an image of him, he became so angry. After all the teaching and trying, they fall back to ignorance, becoming greedy and trying to charm someone.

He said fuck it all and broke all of it. He took them to the holy land; he was full of good intention. But the result was that all the people still prayed to the golden cow.

Q [Another visitor]: In very orthodox Jews, you are not supposed to have any picture in your house...

K: That's why they killed Jesus. They killed Jesus because they claimed that God cannot have any form. That's why I say the only true Buddhists at that time were in Israel at that time. They believed in what Buddha said 'If you meet Buddha on the way, kill him'. But they took it literally, that was a bit strong.

Like in Advaita now they hang the pictures of Ramana, Nisargadatta, UG Krishnamurthy. It never stops; you make idols again. And me sitting in Tiruvannamalai trying to destroy Ramanaism was a joke too because it became a religion and Ramana became the new Jesus for them. And whatever Ramana said became the word of truth. But the main thing is even Ramana said that the truth cannot be spoken – Whatever I say for sure is not true. But now the disciples make him, just as Jesus said and then they made Christianity around him. It's unbelievable, it's unavoidable.

No, they will make you an idol for charming. The normal business of daily life magic needs idols. And if you destroy the idea that they can do something, they make you someone who works for them. It's like devil employs Jesus as a tool and creates a new Church. [Mocking] I will take care about your business down here master. [Laughter] Don't worry, be quiet.

Q [Another visitor]: This concept that magic is permeating every aspect is also mentioned in the course in miracles...

K: Some books have even ninety percent of things that are nice but then there is one percent which says that you can do it. Then they destroy all what was not so bad, they destroy in one little sentence. It's like they would say life is living life – but it is your decision. That is in your hands and by that everything is gone. Fantastic!

Even in the Bible, there would be more than ninety percent I would agree to in basis. But then there are parts in which I will take it and burn it right away. In that sense, I would rather burn every book by just letting it rot in the library where they belong. Even burning them is giving them too much attention.

Q: I like the bones of my most beloved faces...

K: I knew from the beginning that you like cemeteries. Tombstones like cemeteries. I like them too, what's wrong with cemeteries? This is a cemetery here now. Imagine if you could find life somewhere. That's the idea of hell – your idea that you found life. That already is a joke. You claimed to have found life in an imaginary sensational experience of body or spirit. It's a joke. Thank God you can only experience dead. Life can never be experienced. Life has to realize itself, experience itself in dead sensations – dead images. It's all dead! Dead, dead, dead...

The father is dead, the spirit is dead and the son is dead. Only life is alive. The father is not life; the spirit is not life nor is the son.

Q [Another visitor]: All our effort comes back to satyam-shivam-sundaram – truth-godliness-beauty. That is what we try to reach...

K: Yeah. The very intention to reach your nature. You stretch out into eternity and you still cannot find yourself. Jon Duan came back from the beyond and said, 'It's not it, stay where you are'. The best pointer. Ramana said to Papaji, where is your Krishna now? What is not here-now cannot be real. If it is not here, it will never be somewhere else. If you are not now what-you-are, you will not become it in any circumstance.

So, no need to reach out anything. But you will reach out anyway; you cannot stop it. The moment you are awake, you experience the longing of non-experience.

Q [Another visitor]: I had a problem with a western teacher singing bhajans...

K: For a westerner it becomes like when you start to sing in the deep forest so that you are not afraid. It's like charming again. It's like we make a group and then we can talk to each other about things we normally don't talk. You just create a melting pot. When you sing together, you create a similar feeling. You break the armors and open up a bit. Then you feel safe together.

January 27, 2013. First Talk
Koh Samui, Thailand

CHAPTER FOUR

The Real Will Never Be Experienced By Anyone, Not Even By Itself

Q: Who is the one in 'who cares'?

K: That ghost you cannot find. It's an idea. If you look for it, it's gone, not to be found – the care taker. It's just a functioning, when you look at it, it's gone.

Q [Another visitor]: When there's no 'I' thought...

K: When would that be?

Q: Most of the time...

K: No! There is no time without an 'I' thought, so how can there be a time with the 'I' thought? You can call it active and inactive 'I' thought, but the 'I' thought has to be there. The awareness 'I' has to be there. Without the presence there's no time, no experience – nothing.

Q [Another visitor]: Is it possible to have an experience of being real without being an experiencer?

K: No. The Real will never be experienced by anyone, not even by itself.

Q: Is there a possibility to shift in consciousness in a way that it removes the identification and real is there all the time...

K: It's never hidden, that's the problem. There's no second to That what is reality, so it cannot be covered by something else. Reality is all there is, but you cannot experience it because for experience it needs two realities. But otherwise reality is a permanent, absolute experience of 'You are that'. But it's not relative.

Q: When you say it's an experience...

K: It's an absolute experience 'you are'. But there's no 'one' in it, or not in it. You don't even know what-you-are and what-you-are-not. That cannot be attained by someone going or someone coming.

Q: The experience that you just described, which is not an experience...

K: It's an absolute experience. But it doesn't depend on the relative one. It's in the presence and in the absence of whatever you can imagine. The consciousness will always shift to relative, oneness, separation, beyond, prior, all those possibilities. Always a different reference point – that's the nature of consciousness. It cannot stay permanently somewhere. It shifts through all the seven different states through the whole day. Sometimes you are in the personal, sometimes impersonal – absence, presence. Then there's deep-deep sleep in which there is neither a presence of absence or absence of the presence. But you still are what-you-are.

You're permanently shifting. You cannot stay permanently in one place, so you will never find home. There is no final home for you where you can rest. That's the whole point; you will never rest in one thing – absence or presence, impersonal or personal. But your natural state is always what-you-are, it's never lost. There are seven different states of dreaming yourself, but by none of those dream ways, you can gain or lose something.

For the intellect which believes that you are born, all the attention goes to the changes. Then there's always an idea of its better over there then over here and unless I am, what I am, I cannot rest. And I sit here and tell you, you will never rest. What-you-are never needs to rest to be what-it-is. And that what needs to rest to be what-it-is, is a phantom. And if the phantom rests or doesn't rest, let the phantom be concerned about it. But you are absolutely independent of a resting or non-resting phantom.

Q: Sometimes it oscillates to various levels of consciousness that have completely no relation to each other. And I find it completely difficult to relate with this 3D reality. In one level there is the whole which has no separation and then there is this 3D level and both have no relation to each other...

K: When oneness is there, this separation is gone and vice versa. You just shift between differences. When there's relative, there's relative. You shift from one reality to the other one and one is as real as the other one, or unreal – call it whatever. The moment you call it real, you make it unreal. It's just different but in nature it makes no difference to what-you-are – none at all. Because in both of them, you are That – what-you-are. There are different ways of dreaming.

I would say they are just different ways of realizing yourself. They are as real as you are. Maybe there are different ways of realizing yourself and the differences are as real as you are. The reality and realization in nature is not different. There's only Brahman, there's only Reality and there's nothing but That. So, even this [Pointing to the body] is Brahman. This, whatever it is, is what-you-are.

Q: And this goes on endlessly?

K: There was never any beginning and there will never be any end to it. So, whichever way you realize yourself doesn't make you more or less real. That's the only news I can give you. And that what has an idea of more or less reality, or being more or less real, that you can say what Ramana calls it – fleeting, sometimes it's there and sometimes not.

Q: It seems like this reality gets peeled away in layers. But it seems from this space [raising his thumb] when the ideas get peeled bit by bit that, That is all there is...

K: But that's another dimension – the absence dimension. It seems more comfortable there, nothing bothers you.

Q: It can also be excruciating, uncomfortable at the same time...

K: Most people call the emptiness more comfortable as there's no future, no past. Then they found a favorite place and have to make an effort to stay there. They cannot move anymore, they always have to be quiet. At least it's less discomfortable and that's already good enough for them.

Q: It's uncomfortable because it's like a free fall...

K: If you would not fear, there would be no discomfort. But now there's a fear running and then it becomes discomfortable. Then it feels like a free fall, nothing to hold on anymore. Without fear there would be no problem.

Q: But there's a joy of falling at the same time...

K: For one part of you, and then the other part is shitting in your trousers. [Laughter] Both are always there, that's not the problem. One is enjoying every fucking moment – that you cannot find. And the other is always in existential crises and that is always present, that's called the phantom which is always in crises of relative existence – a doubtful 'I'. The 'I' thought is always a doubtful experience of a doubter.

Then there's that what-you-are which cannot not enjoy even that. This schizophrenic experience is permanent. Ramana would say – Abide in that what is always enjoying itself because it doesn't need to enjoy itself. That can never fear itself and the other one will always fear itself. There will always be crises. You may call that consciousness is always inquiring about consciousness and wanting to know if it's real, is it really what I Am. It will always come back. Even when there has been a peaceful time for a moment, it will always jump in – this spider, spinning its network of trying to catch itself. And no way out – that's the phantom actually – the whole consciousness.

Q: How do I know what's true?

K: You can never know what's true. I can only say that whatever has been said is bullshit. But that there can be someone saying and something can be said, you have to be – the unpronounced 'I Am' that you are. This pre-sense, that there can be a presence what-you-are has to be. That's all. The rest, I have no idea. Then we can talk about different presences which are like prisons, different states and dimensions. I call them die-mansions because it's already like a cemetery. It's a dimension of the dead.

Life can never be experienced by life. Whatever life is experiencing is the experience of dead – dead experiences. All the seven states are dead experiences; especially the experiencer is a dead experience. But still that there can be a dead experience, any relative experience, you have to be. And that never becomes more or less by the way these experiences happen, presence or absence or whatever.

All the shifts, all the differences can only be because you are. There's no need to attain that. That's the end of all the exercises of the intellect, there's nothing to argue about it but to abide into that what is doubtlessness that you are, which is always there – this pre-sense which doesn't need to sense itself – the in-no-sense which never needs any sensor sensing differences. It is with and without the sensor. Now we can talk about the sensor because you are awake. The sensor sits here and has a story of sensing. This traveler of senses can now talk about how he traveled through the differences. But this traveler is already a phantom. This sensor, this experiencer with all his stories comes in the morning and is gone in deep-deep sleep, but still you are.

And that is what I would say is your nature and not that what is hunting itself in this realm of dead funerals. So, being what-you-cannot-not-be is not an exercise. It's not an understanding; it's not anything that can be grasped by anything. It never needs to be grasped, never needs to be understood by anything. It's much more than natural to you.

Consciousness will always inquire. This dream of inquiry and seeking never stops – never ever. You cannot otherwise realize yourself as a doubtful experiencer and out of that trying to make the experience real. The unreal, the fleeting will always try to become real. The unreal consciousness always tries to become real, but it will never become real. And that what is real, your nature never needs to become real. There's no between and there's no bridge.

The dream will always be the dream and what is not a dream will always be that what is not a dream. There will be no end in the dream and that what-you-are never started. So, it doesn't need to end, it will never end. There will be no solution in the dream. Whatever solution you find in the dream, whatever answer, will go again. Whatever you realize in this dream, will be a dream realization and the dream realization will be gone sooner or later.

Whatever you understand, whatever you realize is already gone. All these deep insights, all the golden cows of understanding, all that religious bullshit, all that enlightenment, all those things will be – shrppp [making a lightening sound]. For what-you-are, they don't mean anything. They only have a meaning in the dream.

Q: I have been with many teachers and had experiences of God consciousness and cosmic consciousness and suddenly I'm back again and I realize it's all useless...

K: I like that most. That's the infinite story of Buddha. Trying whatever is possible and in the end saying – I am a failure. I tried everything that's possible and had all the possible experiences. Whatever is possible to be experienced, I experienced. But still I failed to know myself. I am the absolute failure, being that what will always fail to know itself.

That's Nisargadatta's ultimate medicine. You try to find yourself in all the rooms and all the dimensions. And in not finding, you find to be that what was never lost.

Q: All this fits perfectly to the absence dimension...

K: But it's still not enough. There's still a little sufferer that knows everything. There's still a doubtful existence.

Q: I wouldn't know where would be the room for that...

K: Even if you cannot find it, it's still there.

Q: It's there when this 3D guy comes in...

K: Even when this 3D guy is not there, it's there. The presence of that one is already hell.

Q: Where could it live there?

K: Everywhere. Even in nothing it lives, even in emptiness it exists. There's no place, there's no dimension, where it's not.

Q: What is it?

K: God's presence. I call it God knowing God, the knowledge to exist. That's the first presence of awareness, the purest notion of 'I', which you cannot experience because in the purest notion there's no experiencer. But even the purest notion of 'I', that's already the phantom. Already that is beginning of hell of differences – very pure, the purest of the purest, pure, pure, pure – unfindable, hidden in some purity.

Q: Even prior to that...

K: Even in the prior. Prior is his last hiding place, he's even hiding in the prior. That's the one who claims – I'm the prior. Fantastic! He's such an asshole, I tell you. He's even hiding in the hole. [Laughter] There are so many infinite traps and tricks. This infinite, absolute intellect hides everywhere. Even in the not hiding, it hides. You cannot get rid of it. It's more than clever. I would call it the devil – God knowing God, he becomes his own devil.

And just by that he knows God; that he's aware to exist, the hell starts. Hell means time – differences. So, even the very purest notion, even in the experience of absence, it's already there. Absence, presence, heaven and hell – all of that. Absence would be heaven, presence would be hell. But even heaven is part of hell and no way out. There's no way out, that's the way you realize yourself.

This is like the Mahabharata, when Yudhisthira was led by Krishna to hell. Is there any tendency of avoidance left? And he was lucky, there was just no tendency left. May there be hell forever – who cares? In this absolute 'who cares', there was neither heaven nor hell. Even Yudhisthira was gone.

This little 'me' is only there because he wants to have a comfortable experience. That it would call enlightenment – I only want to know myself, I'm very innocent in my intention, I only want to know truth, I only want to be whatever. So, he's really a tricky bastard, I tell you – what we call a seeker. In all his facets of seeking, trying to become a special 'apart' devil who knows God. God trying to know himself, already that is the original sin. God becomes a sinner trying to know himself. And the moment he knows himself, he punishes himself that he knows himself – such a punishment, from the beginning. From this first sin [raising his thumb] to know himself, he becomes a relative object of relative knowledge. And by being relative knowledge, he's already punished by not being what he is. By not being what he is, he's longing to be what he is – instantly, just by knowing himself he longs for that what never needs to know itself. What a trick!

Q: It's totally fucked up...

K: That is what-you-are. You are totally fucked up, from the beginning. And no way out! Absolutely, no way out. This is the way you realize yourself – being the seer, seeing, what can be seen – the whole scenery. Being totally fucked up means you are the absolute fucker, the absolute fucking and the absolute fucked. You are the trinity of the fucker, fucking, fucked – father, spirit, son.

Q: When you say – this is the way you realize yourself, what's that?

K: In real-lies – real-lie-zation. This is your realization. Reality, realizing itself in this lie – a lie of separation, a lie of oneness. Whatever you realize, whatever you experience, is a lie. But you are the liar, the absolute liar who's lying to himself in his infinite realization. Who else can lie himself so perfectly and believe in himself? Only you. Who else would you believe and be so stupid to be born? Only because you believe your mother, that is not different from yourself. You believe yourself in your mother. Who else can trap so perfectly? Only you fall in love with an image of yourself. That's your perfect trap. And now you try to get out of that love and that's the next trap. You are fucked, I tell you.

And there was never anyone who came out of it. There was never anyone who made it – never ever.

Q [Another visitor]: So by the tendency to avoid...

K: The tendency to know yourself is the tendency to avoid yourself, the tendency to know yourself as little. You want to avoid the experience of being little. But that is the beginning of all tendencies. You experience yourself as a relative knowledge – the 'I'. And you are trying to avoid that experience of being little.

Q: Then you are trying to hold the 'big'...

K: You want to avoid the little but you don't know what the big even means.

Q: But it has an idea...

K: You only have an idea about the truth. You know what I produce here – no future, no past, not even now. I just show you whatever you try is futile. You failed, you fail and you will fail to know yourself. And I sit here and tell you, be happy about it. If you really could know yourself, that would be hell.

Q: But I have not failed completely...

K: The little successor pops up. That's why you go to workshops that tell you, you can make it. But how can you not fall in love with your image? Even trying not to fall in love is out of love. Now it's too late. Now trying to end this love affair with yourself is too late. Whatever you do is out of love for yourself. So, even suffering comes out of love – this passion for yourself – out of love.

Q: That's impersonal love...

K: But even impersonal love is bullshit.

Q [Another visitor]: Killing love...

K: Marrying is the most famous way of killing love. [Laughter]

Q: Terrorism also comes out of love...

K: Everything comes out of love.

Q: When the experience happens, the self is not there. However, when the experience is over, the self consciousness comes back...

K: It was never gone.

Q: Still 'I Am'...

K: You cannot not be.

Q [Another visitor]: Going of the experience is another experience...

K: Yeah. You just shift. But what-you-are is never shifting. But still there's an experience of a shifter, shifting, whatever can be shifted. Neither shifting nor not-shifting, that's the whole thing. If you say it's not shifting, you make it relative again.

Q [Another visitor]: So, Buddha realized only at a relative level?

K: He realized absolutely that he cannot relatively know himself and absolutely it's impossible because there are no two. So, self can never know the self and whatever the self can know, cannot be the self. The Buddha-nature would never be seen – even by himself. It will never show up, as it's never part of the world. The Buddha never walks the Earth and if you meet Buddha on the way – kill him. Reality can never be seen – anywhere. And no one will ever realize Reality. So, there was never any self-realized person – ever, cannot happen.

And Ramana said the same – There was never any realized person and the Self is ever realized and never needs to realize itself. And there's no in-between. But still people think Ramana is a realized person. From there comes another religion. Buddha would say the same, there was no Buddha, Ramana would say there was never any Ramana. Brahman is all there is and there's nothing else but That. And That is ever realized and doesn't need any special realization and there's no in-between.

The one who needs a special realization is a phantom guest that always claims something. Always hungry, never satisfied, always seeking. That you can call Consciousness. The famous consciousness already is an uninvited guest you cannot get rid of – that's all.

Be what-you-are is in spite of the presence of consciousness trying to know itself. Who cares if consciousness knows or doesn't know itself? Only consciousness. Only phantoms care if the phantoms know or don't know or what phantoms say or don't say. So, if a phantom realizes, it's still a realized phantom. Be generous. You don't even need to destroy them. Just let them believe that they're realized – why not?

Q: So, relatively any experience is just an expression of the Absolute?

K: It's one way of life living life or absolute *Parabrahman*, dreamer dreaming itself.

Q: And that's why any experience, no matter which one, is not it?

K: It is That. The next sip of coffee is as absolute as you are because that is your absolute realization. The moment you realize, you are the realizer realizing what can be realized. So, the next sip of coffee is the absolute realization of what-you-are. So, sitting here you experience the absolute existence realizing itself as sitting here. And this experience of 'sitting here' is as absolute as the experience of enlightenment or the deepest insight. So, having a little fart in our brain is the same realization as the experience of enlightenment. [Laughter] So, all the famous guys who fell from the bench in the park and have this power of now experience; let them have it.

Q: I'm always confused with those examples...

K: Yeah. They try to give you a recipe for happiness and then they claim they made it. But the punishment is that they have to sit with Oprah Winfrey on the same table. [Laughter] That's punishment enough. If someone claims to be special, he's already punished by that. Actually it's all entertainment in that way. It's serious fun.

Q: So, realization is still happening?

K: Moment-by-moment.

Q: It will also go back to the absolute?

K: This is the absolute, there's no going back. When Ramana was asked – When you die where would you go? He responded, where can I go – I am That. How can I go, I never came. Even Jesus said, wherever you lift a stone, I will be there. How can that go what never came? So, going back to absolute is a nice idea. [Mocking] Now, I go back to absolute – bye, bye. I always have fun with people who say my master is in samadhi. He retreated in the absolute and will come back tomorrow. [Laughter] Okay, don't disturb him.

Q: So, the absolute expresses itself...

K: It never expresses itself, that's the problem because then you make it two again. This is not the expression of the absolute, this is the Absolute. That's always the last point that people have, that absolute is potential source and this is just an expression.

Q [Another visitor]: But that's what all the masters have said...

K: Fuck them all. [Laughter]

Q [Another visitor]: Is it not a possibility that it's different than the way you are describing?

K: It's always different but it's still Reality. Reality presenting itself differently is always reality.

Q: So, these guys who say who got it right...

K: I don't say they are wrong or anything. They claim that they have a special experience, not me.

Q [Another visitor]: That's consciousness?

K: Of course, consciousness having a special affair with itself. They claim that one dimension, one space-like awareness, that's more true than this. They give you an advantage state. They make the natural state as a special state that you can reach because they reached it. There was an English lady who said that she didn't feel the energy of Arunachala because she got self-realized before going to Arunachala. She thought she could not feel her energy because she was self-realized but if you are not self-realized you feel the energy. So, she makes a difference. She realized her true nature and the other bloody seekers who go and seek the energy are just bloody assholes. [Laughter]

I just point that how ridiculous it is when one says he has a special realization. I have nothing against them in nature. I just point out the stupidity of consciousness and the stupidity is unlimited. There are no limits of stupidity and ignorance in consciousness.

Q: Maybe...

K: There's no 'maybe'. It's only stupidity. Whatever I say, whatever can be said, whatever they say – it's all stupidity.

Q: Maybe there's also no limit to realization?

K: But Reality can only realize itself in stupidity, it can never realize itself in knowledge. You can only know yourself in relative – whatever. And relative is always relative knowledge and that's ignorance. So, there's only stupidity. Absolute knowledge realizing itself in absolute stupidity. What else?

Q: Can you explain how you know that there's only one valid...

K: Are there two selves?

Q: No...

K: So, the self will never know itself and when the self knows itself, there are two selves and that's ignorance – from the beginning. It doesn't matter in which way it knows itself, it's all stupidity.

Q: But...

K: There's no but in it. Where's the 'but'? There's no 'may be'. May be is only there for the doubtful 'I' who thinks that there's something special because he read so many special books of special people – he thinks, there must be something. This is arrogance that one believes that he doesn't know. This is more arrogance than one claiming that he knows.

Q: Can you say that again?

K: No. [Laughter] You cannot decide, but when you are 'may be', you are 'may be'. Then the 'may be' says 'may be'. Whatever the doubter produces, is a doubtful pronunciation. That's the realm of doubtful experiences. Or you are what-you-are and there's no doubt possible because there's no one who could doubt himself. And there's no bridge between that.

When you are what-you-are, there's a doubtlessness of what-you-are – 'I Am That' and finished, no coming no going, nothing can be added, nothing can be taken away from it. Every moment is as solid and absolute as it can be – Finished!

Q: You said earlier that I cannot rest in the experience of...

K: It will change. The new frame you experience is like a different movie but the other frames that you experience are also there. This movie has infinite frames and it's always finished.

Whatever you say from a 'may be' position, will always be a

'may be' statement that you can doubt and there will be someone who fights against it. There will be discussions and reasonings and all what happens. I Am What I Am and even when I say the biggest stupidity, I am right. That's why people come to me because whatever I say is right. I don't know any wrong; I only know right – by being That what is right.

Q: But I cannot know that...

K: When you talk, you doubt yourself and you make it a doubtful whatever.

Q: I can say that I know things...

K: Yeah. But that's doubtful. I give a shit if I know it or not, I say it anyway. [Laughter]

Q: That's what is happening in this stateless state that I was describing. It's absolute undoubtful...

K: But if you listen to it now, you make it a different state, so it becomes relative. As absolute it seems to be, it's not absolute. The question is who now makes a difference between this and that? Who defines himself here and there?

Q [Another visitor]: Do you say this because it's not-shifting?

K: No. It always shifts but that what is experiencing the shifts, is not shifting. You experience one who is shifting. But that who is experiencing the shifts and the way its shifting, is never shifting. It's uninterrupted solid as it is – never moves. That silence is what is this. This is silence! Nothing comes here, nothing goes here. This realization of reality is infinite in its nature. This infinite now is never born, will never die. This what you call expression is not an expression, it is Reality – never comes, never goes. Nothing is ever born, nothing will ever go. This is Papaji's – Nothing ever happened. It's more like nothing comes in coming and nothing goes in going. Everything is permanently there, whatever can be, is there. All possibilities of Reality are there already in the potential before it ever woke up. It was already fixed – unmovable.

Now being here is as fixed as it was even before it was there – already experienced. That is impossible for the intellect to grasp because there's nothing to do anymore. In that, he cannot survive. There's no here, no future, no past, nothing to do. There's an absolute non-doership there because everything was already done even when it was in potential. Even when it didn't know itself. Even there, everything was already – [Pang] [Makes a sound]

Q: So, would you agree with destiny?

K: But then you make it your destiny, that's the problem.

Q: It's destiny...

K: I don't like the word.

Q: Whether you like the word or not, but that's exactly what you are pointing to...

K: No. I don't point to any destiny. I just point to the Reality which is there – fixed. And Reality has no destiny. I know the tricks of these inner bastards. [Laughter]

Q [Another visitor]: When you say the potential is...

K: I say 'if'. If there would be an absolute potential, all the possibilities, in whatever way the Reality could realize itself, everything would already be happened even before it happens.

Q: But relatively it's limited by time?

K: No. There's no time in it. When all the moments are already there even before they are there, the whole movie is already shot before even the shooting happens. If the script is already finished and it's just an unfolding of an absolute script. That's what Krishna says in *Mahabharata*, the blue print is already fixed and even I cannot change the blue print.

Q: It seems like there are rules in this relative place...

K: Yeah. It seems like when you are born, you have to die. That you can call destiny. The destiny of this body that came out of a vagina has to go back to the infinite vagina.

Q: It also appears that when you go to sleep, there is no movie...

K: Who tells you that? Only because you sleep you think the movie is gone.

Q: You can only go by your experience...

K: You cannot go by anything. Experiences lie all the time, you know that. You believe that you have a body, what an experience! You can become a scientist. Every day I can touch my body, so it must be real, it's like evidence. It's false evidence.

Q: What is the problem in saying that the potential can't express itself totally?

K: It can only express itself totally and not any less than total. Totality can only express itself totally. The Absolute can only realize itself absolutely and not anything less. Everything has to be there, whatever is possible and the impossible. Out of that Absolute potential, there can only be Absolute realization.

Q: So, is it possible that we have this conversation again at that moment I have a white shirt and you have a Pink shirt?

K: No. You will still have a pink shirt and I will have a white shirt. It's absolutely fixed.

Q: So, it's limited?

K: Maybe in one of the other dimension it maybe a different color, but who cares? Even that has to happen. You can say this moment has infinite potential in all directions. There is no limit of one destiny. That's why I say, there's no destiny. All the potential possibilities that can come out of this one are already there too. But the problem is then you say that I choose the more pleasant possibilities. I only want the orange future and not the black future.

Q: And that's pointless?

K: It's pointless. You are That what is realizing itself in all the ways.

So, what difference does it make if you have an orange future or a black future or a green underwear future or a no underwear future? That's why they call it a mind-fuck to make a difference. For what-you-are, it makes no difference. Whatever way – maybe there is, maybe there is not, but who fucking cares? It's all what-you-are, there's no second – that's all. You are That. And you have to fuck yourself, whether you like it or not because there are no others.

If there's sex, you have sex with yourself. There are no others. What else can you experience? You can only be the seer, the seeing, what can be seen in whatever possible ways. You are the penetrator, the penetration, what can be penetrated. You will always imagine an imaginary penetration of yourself. You are the imaginary lingam, the imaginary space and the imaginary information that comes out of it. You are That, in whatever possible or impossible ways. Who gives a fuck if it's one future or millions or billions of infinite futures or pasts? It's all what-you-are.

You are absolute addicted to what-you-are. You are the absolute addict and you are the absolute junkie for yourself. But believing that you can find quality in all of that, then you really become a junkie of a junk idea. This is the quality of existence, of your nature. You are the quality itself, but you cannot find more or less quality. In America it's very famous these days to have a quality time. [Laughter] Then everyone has to spend a lot of attention to candle lights and has to make things expensive because without making it expensive, there's no quality. [Laughter] Your boyfriend cannot take you out Dutch; if he does you will never marry him because there's no quality in him. [Laughter]

But who cares about being stupid? Does it make you more or less as you are? Are you more Self when intelligent? Or are you less Self when you are absolute bullshit and stupid? If you cannot leave yourself anyway, you can be absolutely stupid, and you are That anyway. You are stupid to realize yourself. Buddha calls it a divine accident. It's like an accident, you are not guilty. You fall in love not because you want to fall in love, you just fucking fall in love. That's the nature of falling in love; you cannot avoid it, that's all. If you could avoid it, you would stay in that blissful absence of being prior forever. Fuck you, you have to come back to the next falling in love.

Who would wake up in the morning? You would be happy being in deep-deep sleep forever and ever, no one would come back. By accident, you wake up because something moves and you are awake. Then there's another fucking day in paradise. [Laughter] This is still Adam and Eve and Cain and Able, the polarities. Adam is an archetype of man, God knowing itself. And Eve is the infinite space vagina. Then you have Cain and Able, the polarities of good and bad. And only Able is able to please God by not doing anything. He just gives a shit if God loves him or not. That pleases God. Cain always wants to please God and wants to be the special one and God always punishes him and really gives him a shitty time. So, there are Cains and there are Ables but only Able is able to please God because he gives a fuck about whether God is pleased or not.

This will never stop. Talking about what you don't have to talk about. But why not? That's why I call it sport. When asked, why do you still talk about it if it doesn't make any difference? I say, why not? It's just a sport. Making all the books and all this is just having some interest in yourself, playing with yourself. Like a kid playing. There's nothing to gain in it and nothing to lose in it. This is called meditation – realizing yourself without the expectation that you would ever know yourself. That's the nature of meditation.

But if you become a meditator and do it with a special intention, that's a crime against yourself. Then you get punished by that – you think you are the meditator and by your doing something and famous insights, you can know yourself. That's a punishment already, because you are a criminal. I like to call the ones who meditate as criminals. They should be imprisoned forever and punished and tortured by life, especially bloody meditators. Sitting on an ashram on a stone you would get hemorrhoids forever! [Laughter]

Q [Another visitor]: What is wrong in saying you are my thought?

K: Everything. Because there's an ownership in it. You will be punished for that. One is already punished by owning something, it's crazy. The moment you have something, you have to watch it, so you are already punished by having something. Having a bloody body, you have to brush your bloody teeth even when you know that they will be gone anyway – sooner or later. You have to take a bloody shower every day, no one knows for what. [Laughter] When you smell, you smell fine for yourself. You can never smell bad for yourself. So, you never do anything for yourself, only for your surroundings.

Q [Another visitor]: Would you say this is hell as well?

K: You can say it. I'm always amazed when someone says – Can we say this and this. Yeah, you just said it. [Laughter] What is your question?

Q: Would you say this is hell?

K: No. I just said, this is a paradise.

Q: But it feels like hell...

K: Because you want to be in heaven and you have a special idea of heaven. And because you have a special idea of heaven, this is hell. She wants to have a heaven on Earth, like Eckhart Tolle – The new earth. He wants to create a heaven on earth, a transmutation of human consciousness. [Laughing]

Q [Another visitor]: Without the doubting 'I'...

K: There's no without.

Q: Doubting 'I' and schizophrenia go together...

K: That's why when you meet somebody, you say 'Hello' – it's the lowest hell. [Laughter] Especially when you wake up in the morning – Hello, it's me again. [Laughter] When you wake up there's me, myself and 'I', the trinity. It's not just schizo, the multiple selves wake up. Then there's a competition who rules today – me, myself or 'I'. What's more useful today? If I go to satsang, I stay in the awareness because I may need it later. Or I just go to the 'me' because I have a meeting with my tax agent; I have to meet my enemy. Or I just be myself because I have nothing else to do today. Is that your way of waking up?

Q: More or less...

K: Or what do I cook today for my beloved? [Laughter] How many selves wake up in normal Australian lady?

Q: I don't want to talk to you anymore... [Laughter]

K: I know your true guru is a kangaroo because only guru-can. Can guru? No a guru cannot.

Q [Another visitor]: When you say, be that what-you-cannot-not-be, who are you saying this to?

K: I'm saying it to what I Am. I am saying it to That what never needs anything to be said to.

Q: To be what?

K: Be what-you-cannot-not-be never needs to be addressed. This is a paradox. That's why it's a sport, an entertainment, there's no need to it. That what-you-are never needs to be addressed to; it doesn't need any pointer to be what-it-is. So, what you cannot not be, you are naturally That. It never needs any teaching or a pointer.

Q: So, is that spontaneous?

K: That there can be something spontaneous, you have to be that. Without That, there is no other way of realizing yourself as whatever – spontaneous or not spontaneous. That there can be a dream, you have to be. But you're not prior. Prior is a very clever trap. Maybe in Marathi Nisargadatta never said prior, he may have said – with and without. It doesn't mean that there's something prior because that already implies time. You are with and without – whatever. You are in realizing and in not realizing yourself – what-you-are.

But not prior to something. That's why prior is mis-leading.

But for what-you-are, it doesn't make any difference – misleading or not misleading is actually totally irrelevant. But if we talk about it, it may mislead that there's an Absolute which is prior and beyond something and this is just an illusion. No, this is it!

Q: This is just a screen...

K: That's another illusion because then you say I'm the screen and not the imaginary sensations that dance on me. [Mocking] I'm just this awareness screen. I'm like the sky and the clouds coming from the left and on the right. I'm just space-like awareness and there's a sensational dance of energetic emotions from the left and the right but I am unmovable in that. It always sounds profound and everyone says – 'me' too. [Laughter] Please, how can I reach that? How many seminars do I have to attend to be that? How many vipassana exercises? How do I step into the air softly and become that awareness? [Laughter]

Any questions?

Q: I'm sure there are more...

K: It never stops. Why should you be better off than me? I have to sit here and talk too. It's just like you come here as a 'why' and I sit here as a 'why not'. That's all what happens here. There's always variations of why and variations of why not.

Q: Lately I've become reclusive and only knew one person I could talk to, that's why I'm here...

K: You lose all the relative companies like friends, they become more and more pale. The best is you cannot decide anything, it's already decided. No one to blame, not even God or yourself. No guilt, no sin. That's quite peaceful.

Q [Another visitor]: But we have to make plans...

K: If you want God to love you, you have to make plans. That's why this is called plan-it (planet) earth. This is a big plan of God here and even he cannot make it different. This almighty bastard who does not have any energy. He cannot change anything. What an omnipotence he is and what an impotent bastard in action. Isn't that fantastic! When he vibrates he has to vibrate in an absolute manner. He cannot vibrate just a little bit. In one big bang, the whole milky way comes out. [Laughter] That's really a free willy!

Q [Another visitor]: When you say you have a doubtful existence, is that Am I – I Am?

K: No. That's the pronounced 'I' – the pronouncer. There's an unpronounced 'I Am' and when it starts to pronounce itself, like a pronouncer pronouncing what can be pronounced, the pronouncer has to exist. That's when existence starts. That you can already doubt. By that movement, by that experience, you become a pronouncer or the creator. Already there you are a doubtful existence because as a creator you are different from what you create – from the beginning. That's the root thought 'I', the creator thought, God knowing God.

The moment God knows God, it becomes a doubtful God – the instant doubter. God knowing God becomes two Gods, that's like God becomes his own devil. He creates his own hell from that doubting place. Instant doubt, instantly two. The moment God knows God, there are two Gods. Then it becomes bi-god (bigot). That's the nature of hell where the time starts. You realize yourself in separation, in two. You cannot prevent falling in love with the first existence because you are not different from it. That becomes your reality. Your reality is a doubtful reality. From there on, you want to end that doubt. You don't know what you long for, but you long for the absence of the doubtful existence.

So, in the presence, you long for the absence. Any presence is longing for the absence. The 'me' is permanently longing for the absence of the 'me'. That's the first enemy. Any 'me' is the enemy because there the war starts. You start to conquer again but you don't even know what. The inquiry starts, the lover starts. The lover out of being in love with itself longs to know itself. The lover loving the beloved in all possible ways. But he cannot find the beloved. He could never find himself in any relative experience, but he tries – out of love for himself.

You can have many perspectives of that – call it love, call it intention, call it longing for absence, call it whatever. That's already like a seed when God knows himself and you cannot avoid it. That will always happen. God becomes aware and from that awareness – consciousness starts and consciousness will always inquire into itself. No way out! That's consciousness seeking consciousness.

Ramana would say – How can the absolute seek the absolute? But look – it happens, why not? The self looking for itself. It's a joke, but it happens. Shit happens! You never lost yourself but you still believe in the idea that you lost something and you want to gain it back. You have an experience of losing, but nothing is lost. I don't deny the experiences of losing. But experiences are false evidences. It's all false, a false going out and the false going back. No one ever went out and no one can ever go back. But you try.

Whatever you experience is false and you know that by absolute intuition. By nature you know that. There's knowledge that this cannot be it. But you cannot stop it. You have to be what-you-are in spite of that. There's an absolute intuition, knowledge of your nature which knows this is not it.

But maybe the idea of 'me' means that you can only be That without that; that you have to get rid of this. But I tell you, you cannot get rid of your realization. You have to realize yourself, if you like it or not – in whatever possible ways. And Ramana said the same, you have to realize yourself. But for sure, everyone takes it personal and says – Which self do I have to realize? Then you want to go back somewhere and say – where is my fucking self?

No! He already talks to reality itself, to what-you-are. What-you-are is Reality and you have to realize yourself. You cannot not realize yourself. There's no way out for you. And the worst part of realization is being a human, having a body, this disease and having a destiny of dying. That's the worse but this is one Absolute aspect of your Absolute realization and you cannot avoid it. If you cannot be here now, in this so-called lowest of the lowest – being a human asshole what-you-are – you will not become in any other. [Laughter]

So you rather be here what-you-are here because you will not become it any special space. The moment you are in that special space, you are gone for me. I cannot reach you anymore. I can only talk to you when you are here and you can only be what-you-are, here-now. When you are in that realm of space-like thing – you are already out of reach. Bye, bye. [Laughter]

Here! If you cannot be what-you-are as this what you call hell of relative experiences, of having this disease body around you, always having to feed this bastard and all of that. If you cannot be what-you-are in the worst case scenario of this having a human experience, with all the drama of relationships and fathers and mothers and all the emotional asshole bullshit fucking you from all around. [Laughter] If you cannot make it with all the family constipation – what-you-are – you will not become it anywhere else. And this will always wait for you.

So, may it be as it is. You are fucked anyway. This is the lowest fuck, but then you want to uplift the spirit and fuck higher. [Laughter]

Q [Another visitor]: So, in you there's a fulfillment experience that is not depending on anyone or anything?

K: No. I'm absolutely happy that I don't have to be happy to be what I Am. I absolutely enjoy that I don't have to enjoy to be what I Am. I don't need joy, that's the nature of joy. Whatever peace can be experienced – peace-off. To be that what never needs any peace to be what-it-is. So, peace-off or joy-off or do whatever, consciousness.

What-you-cannot-not-be, you are in any given dream or not-dream, call it whatever. That is absolutely in spite of all whatever you can imagine or not imagine. When you want to become it, it's hell. When you are it, it's neither hell nor heaven. But the moment you want to become it, you fuck yourself so deep and it hurts so much. This longing for That, by trying to become what-you-are, it's such a fucking hell for every fucking moment when you are not what-you-are. And you are punished by that, just by trying to become what-you-are. In trying to know yourself, you make it a relative object of whatever can be known. That's already a punishment.

You don't need any God; you don't need any devil to punish you. You punish yourself and only you can punish yourself so deeply and so profoundly as no one else can punish you. That's the original sin, when God knows God. He becomes a sinner because then he becomes a doer, a creator and from there on he wants to justify what he has not done. That's judgment day, always trying to justify what he has not done, but he claims to have done.

That's the little doer bullshit that wakes up in the morning and asks himself what did I do yesterday or what I should have done. [Mocking] It depends on me whether the world is a heaven and hell and I do all the good deeds. Always having this moral and ethical stand-point. All this fucking around with all you have to be, all this religion is made out of hell. Only the devil takes care about this planet.

Q [Another visitor]: But it is the existence creates longing...

K: Existence longs for the absence of existence, it doesn't create it. Now you want to blame someone. I know you. [Laughter] I'm sitting here because I know all the tricks and I know them by heart. I invented them. [Laughter]

Q: Does the existential fear come from longing?

K: It's a false evidence of existence. Fear is four lettered – False Evidence Appearing Real. Then the believer becomes real because there's a false evidence of existence appearing real. And from that false evidence, there's fear. From there the whole fucking starts, trying to get out of fear. The tendency is to get rid of the fear. The tendency is wanting not to exist. You want to kill something. So, every spiritual seeker is trying to get rid of what-you-are.

Q: And the tendency of longing comes?

K: It doesn't come. It's just that the nature of any relative existence is fear. It's a doubtful existence. But it's a false evidence, that I can point to.

Q: So, there's nothing wrong with fear?

K: It's all wrong. It starts wrong and it ends wrong. Out of false only false can come. The false appearance creates false results.

Q: So, when fear comes...

K: There is no coming, it's already there. When you exist, there's already fear.

Q: So, there's no getting away from it? You are the fear?

K: You are not the fear. You experience yourself in fear, but you are not the fear. The moment you know yourself as whatever, it's doubtful. Then you want to get rid of that doubt because you fear that you have to know yourself to be yourself.

Q: That happens to me...

K: It happens to the whole world. The whole consciousness has a why-rus (virus) inside – Why? Why? Why? That's a virus – this disease of 'why'. Then I sit here as an antidote – why not? Does anything happen when you experience fear? It's a false evidence.

Q: So, relax?

K: Relax is too much. [Laughter] You cannot get more relaxed than you already are because as you are that without a second, there's not even a possibility of a relaxation and no need for it. Only a relative bastard needs relaxation. So, relax! You don't have to relax! [Laughter]

Q: We keep following you as an antidote...

K: Why not? I can just repeat what I said as Nisargadatta and Ramana – the disease came and the disease will be gone. Then another disease comes. [Laughter] It's called the dis-ease. The ease you are, you cannot lose and you cannot gain. You can only experience yourself in diseases, in discomfort. There's no other way of experiencing yourself other than discomfort.

Compared to the Absolute whatever, everything else whatever you experience, even the most comfortable circumstance is discomfort. The ease of what-you-are, you will never experience. Whatever you can experience is a discomfort of two. There will always be a discomfort and there will always be a doubt. And I tell you be happy about it that you cannot find peace or ease anywhere. So, peace-off. Who needs bloody peace? Or being at ease. Who can be at ease? When there is ease, there is no one who can be at ease and that one who can be at ease, is a fake one.

February 6, 2013
Mumbai, India

Chapter Five

The Peace You Can Get, Peace-Off
~

Q: Nisargadatta says the spirit is a sport and likes to overcome obstacles. That's why all things are happening...

K: Yeah, without obstacles it would not work. It plays dumb. It does 'as if' there is something. It has to make itself blind to experience. How otherwise can man have a relationship with a woman? [Laughter] Or a woman have a relationship with man? You do 'as if' you get something out of it. Actually you know by heart that you can get nothing by it. But still you try – just-in-case. All the things that happen are just-in-case. You believe in God just-in-case there's one. You really don't know if there's really one or not. Praise the Lord – just-in-case.

Just-in-case: you marry, just-in-case: you go to church, just-in-case: you work and just-in-case: you buy a new television set – just-in-case it 'maybe' makes you happy. It's all maybe and the little hope never dies. That one day a guru, an event, an enlightenment, that's all just-in-case – maybe it makes me happy. The highest would be enlightenment – just-in-case it helps. That makes one a nut case. Otherwise it would not continue like this.

Q: Otherwise there's no movement...

K: There's no movement at all, that's the whole problem. It doesn't need any movement. It's a solid block of realization – already done. That what *Parabrahman*, that dream is already dreamt. It never needs any movement. From a relative point of view, you can say that without that there will be no attraction, no tendencies, no expectations and all of that. But from the Absolute, everything is done already and doesn't need any movement. But if you want to understand it in this way, that it is natural, then you can understand it like that.

Q: What happens to the Reality that I Am when the body stops functioning? Where does it go? I am something that I do not know what I am other than body and mind.

K: But you exist! So you cannot say you do not know what-you-are. That's the knowledge you are. That you can say that I don't know what I Am, you can only say because you know that you are. The knowledge of 'I Am' that you-are, there's nothing more to it. That you can say 'I don't know', you have to be what-you-are and that already you know. There's knowledge, the knowledge that you are, the knowledge of I Am – unpronounced – without which no one who can pronounce that 'I don't know'. So, you have to know. So, you lie already when you say 'I don't know'. I just catch you as a liar.

Q: But What I Am, I don't know...

K: That you cannot know, you have to know that you-are. There's nothing more to it, that's knowledge. You don't need to know more to be what-you-are. That you can claim not to know, you have to be that. That's Ramakrishna's basic pointer.

Q: What happens when the body is no more?

K: Nothing happens! That what is the I Am is always there and the body comes and goes. But the I Am stays; it's unmovable – never comes and goes. So, nothing happens when it comes and nothing happens when it goes. It doesn't make you more to have a body and doesn't make you less not having a body. The knowledge of 'you are' is inspite of presence or absence of any body. So, nothing happens. Nothing comes in coming and nothing goes in going. But now you believe that you have to worry about what will happen when this body is gone.

Q: My brother died recently and his body stopped functioning...

K: The piece of meat is gone, but your brother is not gone. You never had any brother. How can what-you-are have a brother? [Pointing to questioners brother] He is not your brother there and you are not his sister. [Laughter] Do you really want to have a brother like him? [Laughter]

You are not sad that your brother died, you are sad that you lost something. But you don't even know what you lost. You lost an idea. Oh, there was something, people tell me I should be sad now. What happens if I'm not sad? Am I bad person? Am I not a good sister if I don't suffer that my brother died? Maybe you don't feel the pain of the loss; would that make you a bad sister? A bad family member?

Q: What goes out of the body?

K: There's nothing in the body. What's in the body? Food. [Laughter] Nisargadatta says food body. What is in the body? Food. What comes out of the body? Please say it for me.

Group: Shit! [Laughter]

When this body gets burnt, the shit gets burnt. That's why the famous – shit happens. Shit comes, shit goes. Knowledge, *chit* always remains as it is. The knowledge that you-are – *chit* – which is your nature is never effected by that coming and going, fleeting ideas and images. That is *chit* and this is relative shit. You always look into shit and expect to get *chit* out of it. It's impossible to get *chit* out of shit. Thank God you cannot find *chit* in shit.

You cannot find the knowledge you-are in relative experiences. The relative experiences come and go and nothing happens. So, what to do? Just be what-you-cannot-not-be and that is *chit*. But now you give attention and expect to be happy from this fleeting – whatever.

I sit here and tell you that be happy that you don't get happy by one of that. If you would get satisfied by one of these events, by whatever understanding, by whatever sensational experience, you would depend on it. Your joy, your nature is never depending on all those dream experiences.

So, be happy that you don't get happy by one of that. You get sad because nothing makes you happy and I tell you be happy that nothing makes you happy. I just turn it totally around. But I know it's not so easy because you fall in love with that piece of meat. Every morning it's there, so it becomes like evidence that it exists. But it's false evidence. Just because it comes every morning, it doesn't make it more or less real. It changes every day – you know that. First you are a baby and now it's totally different. Every seven years all the cells are different. So what do you claim to be? Changing what? Always new cells, new clusters and functioning of cells. Then there are the wrinkle cells and the non-wrinkle cells. What are you the wrinkle or the non-wrinkle? Everyone wants to be the non-wrinkle and not the other half of the face.

Q: So, what is Reality? Is it energy?

K: If I would know what is Reality, I would tell you. But thank God I don't have to know what is Reality because Reality is already an idea. If you call it Reality, you make it an idea. So, you better don't know what-you-are and what-you-are-not. The moment you call it something, you make it different to something else and then you already make it shit.

'You are' – that's all. But you will never know what that is. But if you call that Reality, then the rest is not Reality. Then you are already separated from something else. Just be what is inspite of all whatever you can imagine. Just be inspite, not because. But that what is inspite; no one needs to know because there's no one who needs to know anything. And that one who needs to know something would always need relative fleeting experiences and understandings which come and go with this body. If this hard-disk is gone, all the precious things are gone with it. If the cow is gone, the 'holy' cow is gone with it. [Laughter]

So, what to do? We are talking about happiness. [Laughter]

Q: But I was troubled a lot when my brother passed away...

K: Yeah because everyone then faces his own death because it's coming closer. You are of the age of your brother and then you think – Oh, I'm already the next one. If he can die, I can die too.

Q: That's one aspect. At the same time, you feel the loss...

K: No. You feel self pity. What else? Poor me, I lost my brother. It's like poor me, someone stole my car, poor me I don't get more money from my company, poor me I don't get this – poor me. It's not about your brother, I tell you. It's only poor me. That's really not so nice.

Now you have a problem, you own this body. Then you already imagine what would happen if I lose that body. So, you already suffer about a loss that may happen in whatever future. You have a psychological problem that you own something and now you fear to lose it. What an idea! An imaginary ownership and then an imaginary loss. Isn't it crazy?

Ownership is suffering; you know that – from the beginning. Look, by having a body, you have to take care about it. Ramana calls having this body as a disease, an illness. It comes to you; it will be gone one day. So, it's already gone. Actually everyone should be happy if someone dies.

Q: But are we afraid of our own death?

K: Who's afraid? Say 'me'. The 'me' that comes with the body is afraid that the 'me' cannot be without this body. That's his problem, the 'me' problem. Wherever 'me' is there's a problem because 'me' means mine – my life, my body, my, my, my. This ownership, that's 'me'. Just be what-you-are and by that you drop all the ownership at once. That's the direct being what-you-are. But trying to devote something and surrendering something, that's an infinite job, I tell you. By understanding, trying to get rid of a falsity, that's called karma yoga and that goes on forever. You can never lose enough and you can never devote enough. And who devotes the devoter? The devotee. Who then devotes the devotee? Everyone says I gave up bhakti – Ha, ha, ha. Everyone gives up what never belongs to him. I gave up so much, I gave up that thing, I donated so much, I dropped all the beliefs – 'me'. First they are proud that they have something and then they are proud that they donated it somewhere.

Q [Another visitor]: There seems to be an apparent separation...

K: Apparently. But only apparently, not really.

Q: So, what's the difference in terms of knowledge between the one that speaks and the one that listens?

K: There are many who ask 'why' and here there's one who says 'why not'. All the people who come wanting something have the main question – why? And I just have the one and possible answer – why not? That's all. That makes me sit here and the others sit there. Why's are many and the why not's are not so many.

Q: So, there's no learning happening here?

K: No, absolutely not. If at all, there's an unlearning. If at all there's something happening, it's destroying of all what you have learned. Just like bubbles exploding moment by moment. The bubbles of ownership, owning this, owning that, being born, bubble, bubble, bubble. And after a while you just enjoy that there would be infinite bubbles. You cannot destroy every concept because even destroying is a concept.

So, you may enjoy the ride of entertainment of existence. It was created once and now it gets destroyed. But in both, nothing happens.

Q: But there seems to be the one who asks – why seems to want to get to a position of why not. There's a progression that one looks for, that's seeking...

K: That he comes to the point of Buddha where he had to say that I'm the absolute failure. He tried absolutely everything and failed to know himself. He said, by whatever I tried, by going deeper and deeper, higher and higher, by whatever experience of depth and truth, I cannot know myself. If it's all futile the whole attempt, then there's a natural peace, which was always there. But you are just giving attention to fleeting shadows and it seems like you lost your peace. But that was only an imaginary losing. Then an imaginary gaining it, by seeing that all the experiences are fleeting.

You are the peace you are – you were, you are and you will be which is not depending on any experience in front of you. That's normally called realization or enlightenment – that you can never know yourself. That you can never be enlightened. That's the dropping of the unenlightened one. But that doesn't make you an enlightened one.

Q: There's nothing you can do to make that happen?

K: No. It will happen by its own course. It's already happened because whatever came to you – the veil, will be gone one day. There were two sadhus sitting under a tree and one was complaining that they were not enlightened. Then Narad comes and the sadhu asks him – When would I get enlightened? As many leaves as there are in the whole forest, you will need those many life times to get enlightened. Then the sadhu starts whining. Then Narad says the same to the other sadhu and he gets ecstatic – I will get enlightened! Who cares when?

That's the question – who cares when? If it will happen in whatever time, it has already happened now. So, why worry about it? You can enjoy the ride until then. Because what else is there to do? If it happens anyway, you can put down your luggage and enjoy the ride. That's the pointer. So, the ignorance came to you and one day it will be gone. Then you are already what-you-are, because you are what-you-are without that.

Q: Are you saying that ignorance itself is the illusion?

K: Yeah. Even knowledge is an illusion.

Q: It's not true?

K: I have no idea. If you ask me, I can only say that there's an absolute absence of any idea of what I am and what I am not. This absence of any presence of one who knows or doesn't know, I would say is my natural state. That what's the nature of what I Am, which I cannot-not-be because I Am that in deep-deep sleep and I am not That. So, it's not something that I gained or lost something. What I Am doesn't know what-it-is and what-it-is-not. There's an absolute absence of one who knows or doesn't know – that is what I Am. And the rest is the rest.

But in that rest, you cannot rest. You can only rest in that where no one needs to rest. That's the nature of rest. But in the so-called presence of one who is looking for rest, for peace, there will never be any peace. There will maybe a temporary rest, landing somewhere, then you depart again. So, you would never get peace. The peace you can get, you can say peace-off. I Am what I Am without whatever you can imagine. Even peace becomes an idea in that. So, forget it.

Then I have to tell you that because you are what-you-are, you have to realize yourself. You cannot not realize yourself. You are already That what is reality and that what is nature of life has to live itself in all possible ways, you cannot stop it. *Parabrahman* the absolute dreamer has to dream. He cannot stop dreaming. Life has to live life – since the beginning and the end, there will never be any end to it.

So, it's not as if you have to realize your true nature. You are already what-you-are and now you have to realize yourself – if you like it or not, in whatever possible way. And I like the word realize because they are real-lies. The liar, the lying and what can be lied. In that way, you realize yourself. First as a liar – God knowing God is already a liar. He knows himself as a lie. Then lying is the spirit and what comes out of it is what can be lied. The false creating false.

So, you can only experience yourself as false. You can never experience yourself as what-you-are. Fantastic! That's the best. False, false, false. It starts false and it gets false. Falsity – from the beginning till the end. That I call entertainment. And you cannot get rid of it. [Laughing]

Q: So, what is it that begins the seeking?

K: Love makes you start seeking. You fall in love with an image of yourself and then you start seeking. You become a narcissist. Awareness is the first mirror of your existence. By waking up there is awareness and then there's an instant love at first sight. So, God falls in love with an image of God – with the first notion of 'I'. There's a lover already. And the lover by longing wants to know the lover. That's all what you can experience in the whole consciousness. God as a lover longing to know himself. The whole universe is made by that. The whole existence, whatever you can experience is a love of God – for himself and it will never end.

Q: So, there's no 'I' that's longing for itself?

K: There's an idea. God as an idea longing for truth. The unreal God longing to become real or longing to know his Reality. But the unreal God can never know his Reality. The unreal will always be unreal, there's no way out. So, whatever the unreal God is experiencing are unreal experiences. Because the unreal is already an unreal experience. There's no way out of that. No escape.

What-you-are never needs anything and that what-you-are-not will always try to become what-it-is. But it will never become what-it-is. The beauty of it is it's already what-it-is. The joke is permanent. I try to explain you God's love for itself, but it's just a helpless explanation. I don't claim it's true. It may calm you down and by seeing you that it's love of God and by that you may rest. But even that, is a concept.

That's why I say you better be what-you-cannot-not-be which

is what-you-are in deep-deep sleep. You were, you are and you will be – uninterrupted. And that what needs an explanation, it sounds good – that's all. But it's not sound enough for what-you-are. So, nothing will ever be sound enough. No explanation, no understanding will ever satisfy you. Temporarily – maybe, but not for long.

Q: And the seeking stops even if there's no understanding?

K: Every night it stops and every morning you pick it up again. And death is another stop. With death it stops and with birth it starts again. But every night it stops and every morning the seeker wakes up. Then the disease happens because there's an experience of dis-ease, a discomfort. Then you seek a way out of discomfort – that's all. It's a natural longing for comfort, a way out of discomfort because every presence is a discomfort because every presence is relative. It's like an image; it's sometimes there, sometimes not. So, you long for something that's not temporary and that will never stop.

So, consciousness will never stop inquiring – no way. Because consciousness already is a phantom. And the phantom always permanently tries to become real and tries to know itself.

Q [Another visitor]: Is the knowledge 'you are' also an illusion?

K: The knowledge you can talk about, is an illusion. That 'you are', you don't have to call it anything. But if you call it knowledge, it's already an illusion because you have to pronounce it. And the knowledge you can pronounce, is already a concept – just a word. If possible, I would not call it anything. But if you want to call it something, just call it knowledge. I would rather call it underwear – un-aware and aware. I am even the underwear of the underwear.

Q: But the knowledge 'you are' is the awareness?

K: No. Awareness already is known. So, it cannot be knowledge. You can talk about awareness, so it can be known and what can be known cannot be knowledge. The knower can be known, the knowing can be known and awareness is part of what can be known – experienced. So, it cannot be the knowledge.

Knowledge cannot experience knowledge. There are no two knowledge's. The knowledge you can experience is relative, it's not the knowledge we are talking about. The energy can never experience energy. The energy you can experience is a reaction of that energy, but not energy.

Q: Echo?

K: Echo in what?

Q: Reflection?

K: It's not a reflection. In what? Then it would already need time that reflects it.

Q [Another visitor]: So, the knowledge you-are is a fact?

K: It's neither a fact nor an effect because if you make it a fact, the effect is different from the fact. That cannot be. Then the reaction is different from the action. So, you even make the action as a reaction. There is no origin; there is no source from where something comes out. That's an illusion. There's only Brahman, there's only energy, energy experiencing itself. But even the most stupid sensation in its nature, is energy.

So, you are not the way you experience yourself, you are always that what is experiencing yourself – as a knower, knowing, what can be known. But you are not the knower, you are not the knowing, you are not something what can be known. You are That Absolute knower who knows himself as knower, knowing, what can be known. As aware, conscious and unconscious – you are That what realizes itself in whatever possible way and you are not different than what you realize yourself as. If you make the fact different from the effect, then you make two again.

Q [Another visitor]: But 'I know' or 'I Am' is a fact, isn't it?

K: If it would be a fact, there would be no 'isn't it'. A fact has to be without any doubt.

Q: I exist is a fact...

K: No. Even that is doubtful, doubtful pronouncing. Whatever you pronounce, you doubt and can be doubted. If you don't doubt, someone else will doubt it for you. No way! You can say, that there can be a doubter, doubting what can be doubted, you have to be – whatever that is. But the moment you say it, you make it doubtful again. So, if you don't want to make it doubtful, you stay quiet. But even that is doubtful. [Laughter] Then there's one who is quiet – a quiet doubter.

You cannot get out of it as much as you try. Whatever you do or don't do, you are doubtful. Saying it or not saying it is too late. So, the pronouncing it or not pronouncing it, the pronouncer already is false. The pronouncer pronouncing or not pronouncing, whatever he's pronouncing or not-pronouncing – is false.

That's why the doer, doing or not doing – both is false. But everyone takes that as an understanding. It's all God's will but I'm not doing anything – you still make these differences. But it was never meant like that. Absolute non-doership means that there is not even a God that does anything. Nothing is ever done and nothing will ever be undone. It's more like a pointer to – nothing ever happened. Life never comes, life never goes, that's all. And life is all there is – call it Brahman, call it whatever. There's no coming in coming and no going in going. So, nothing ever happened. That's no-time because nothing no coming in coming and no going in going. That's no two.

I know it's impossible to understand and that I like. Because you cannot understand and put it in your pocket and take it home. That's the beauty of your nature, it cannot be owned by anyone. Not by any understanding, not by any experience, any whatever you claim to know or not to know, is absolutely impossible. So, whoever claims that he realized his true nature, you are facing a liar.

That's the beauty, there was never any realized person on earth – never was, never will be, never ever. As in the first place, there was no unrealized person. How can out of that unrealized person which was not there, a realized person come? First show me one who's unrealized and then we can talk about it.

But then always comes – what about 'me'?

Q: So, what-you-are is beyond nothing and everything?

K: No. I didn't say that. Beyond is already separation again. I like Nisargadatta, if you want to say something, just say – I Am That – finished. That means you don't know but it means that you don't have to know – I Am That – finished. In the Bible it says, I Am That I Am – finished. But beyond already is an understanding and is a misunderstanding. Prior is an understanding, is a misunderstanding. I say – with and without whatever – 'you are'. But that's also a pointer.

Q [Another visitor]: In the earlier books, Nisargadatta said, reside in the 'I Am'. But in the later books he talked about transcending the 'I Am'...

K: Yeah, transcending the seven states. Even the 'I Am', you have to transcend by being the 'I Am'. Transcending the 'I Am' is being the 'I Am' not knowing any 'I Am'. By that you transcend everything. It's the easiest you cannot do, that's the problem.

Q: In The Ultimate Medicine he said – Who is aware of the 'I Am'?

K: That he calls it the 'I Amness'. The 'I Amness' already needs one who is aware of the 'I Amness' But the unpronounced 'I Am' is not what one can be aware of because that what you can be aware of, it's already too late. So, the 'I Am' that you can be aware of is 'I Amness' which is already a dream. But the nature of 'I Am' doesn't know any 'I Am'. And by being that what-you-cannot-not-be, you transcend all that can be transcended – even the transcender is transcended.

So, by transcending the transcender, by being what-you-are, it's totally impossible that there can be someone or not. You transcend everything at once. In a split second, everything is destroyed. In being what-you-are, you destroy all illusions, all ignorance at once, just by being what-you-are. By being the knowledge that doesn't know anything, never needs anything to be what-it-is. By that, you destroy the destroyer and the creator – at once.

Being Shiva itself not knowing Shiva and seeing the light already as a dream. The light of Shiva is not Shiva. The awareness of Shiva is not Shiva. Shiva never knows himself as Shiva. But the moment Shiva knows Shiva as the light of Shiva, the dream starts. But there Shiva ends. Where Shiva starts, Shiva ends.

The moment you know yourself, there are two. When God knows God, he's his own devil. He creates his own separation. But he cannot help himself, he cannot not start it. So, shit happens – even for God. I forgot, says God. I don't know what is God, but I forgot, says God. It's all too late. Now you have to realize yourself in all that stupidity, if you like it or not. You have to be inspite of all whatever you call discomfort of knower, knowing, what can be known – you-are. You cannot make it undone, what is never done. But you try and that makes you a seeker. You try to undo something that was never done. Nothing ever happened but you try to undo that.

You never knew yourself, but now you want to make it undone. Even by the understanding that knowing yourself is bad because as soon as you know yourself, the false starts, it doesn't make any difference. Because by that, you cannot get rid of it. What a joke!

Q [Another visitor]: So, the exhortation to know yourself is a joke in itself?

K: Yeah. It's an entertainment. But sometimes you don't understand your own joke, that's the problem. [Laughter] And then you are very pissed about yourself. And then you want to kill that bastard who made this joke. Then you become a revengeful God, an angry

God. Everyone feels this anger in himself – Why did God put me in this position? Even when you realize that you are that God who is realizing himself, even that doesn't make you less angry. How can I ever bullshit myself like this? In Bible there are so many stories about the anger of God or the revenge of the jealous God. The moment he knows himself, he is jealous about the God who doesn't know himself. The God who knows God is jealous about the God who doesn't need to know God – already. What a drama! Shakespeare is nothing against God's own drama. When Rama knows Rama, he becomes a drama-queen.

Nisargadatta is one of the rare guys who says that you have to transcend all the seven states of relative samadhis – just by being what-you-are, you have to transcend all of that. And as long as you have not transcended and you are still landing in one of them, you are still an ignorant bastard. It's very rare. Only Ramana and Nisargadatta are the ones I know who talked about the seven states and that you have to transcend them, just by being what-you-are. The moment you are in one of that prior state or any state of samadhi, you are still an ignorant bastard. But even they have to make money.

Q [Another visitor]: What about the landing?

K: It's a pilot with a plane. He has a plane and then he has to land somewhere. It's a stupid pilot with a plane. It's like you having a body and now you are looking for a place to rest. Then you are the pilot of a spirit. Then you are the pilot of something else but you are always looking for an advantage landing place. And for sure, you look for a landing place, where you can rest forever.

You look for peace everywhere. You look for the peace in the body, then you look for the peace in the spirit and then you look for peace in the prior. But all the peace you can find is temporary; it will be gone one day. If you cannot be here-now in this 'asshole' position and it's really an asshole position. I mean it. By having an ass, you are an asshole owner. If you cannot be what-you-are in that asshole position, you will not become it one of the other states. If you cannot be here-now, you will not become it.

Q: So, you can't crack the illusion?

K: Of course you can crack the illusion just by being what-you-are. You always have to make an effort to keep the illusion alive. Just be the laziest bastard you are. [Laughter] You just work too much, you are too German.

Q: I thought you said you cannot make it longer or shorter?

K: Of course you can make it absolutely shorter by being what-you-are. Just be what-you-are and the phantom will still continue to seek.

Q: So I step out?

K: You cannot step out. By no way out, you are just what-is.

Q: So, I can step out buying into the dream?

K: That's again trying to land in a stepping out landing place. Your tricks are infinite, I know. The phantom's tricks are infinite, as the intellect is. The mind intellect has its infinite tricks and traps. It's full if infinite and unlimited tricks. You always find a reason for jumping from there to there and jumping up and down.

No. It will never end. When I said before that it will end one day, I lied. [Laughter] Now I say the opposite. [Laughing] That's what I like; I don't have to stick to the bullshit I said half an hour ago. I just change it and make another approach of whatever kind. I just employ everything and I just forget the shit I said before. Then I forget this one again. Just adjusting, when I talk to you I say different things than when I talk to someone else.

I don't have a teaching; I don't have to stick to some bullshit. So, it will never end for you. [Laughter] For the others it will end, but not for you. [Laughter] I'm a bastard and I like it.

Q [Another visitor]: So, what you are pointing is That is landing...

K: Only the phantom can land. What-you-are never started.

Q: The phantom is not landing...

K: The phantom is always landing. The phantom without landing somewhere is not a phantom. The phantom needs a concept of where he can land, like having a body or having a life. It needs to own something, like landing. If one is landing in the prior, he owns the prior. If someone lands in a body, he owns the body. If someone lands in the spirit, he owns the spirit.

Q: It's That which owns it, not the phantom...

K: The phantom is the owner. But who owns the phantom? Who knows? Or do you have an idea? [Laughter]

Q [Joking]: It's completely stupid that I have been sitting with you for so long hoping you had an idea...

K: You can only experience that I jump from one to another and I give a shit. I have no personal ideas. I just pick them up and throw them away again. As I say, I don't need a sound teaching which I can repeat day by day and you can follow that. I am more than slippery. The moment you think you got me, I'm already somewhere else. Catch me if you can.

Q [Another visitor]: You say just be what-you-cannot-not-be...

K: You are. Just be that.

Q: But somebody has to do that?

K: No. I don't talk to that somebody. You take it personal, I never talk to you. I don't even know your name. I don't need names. That's why I call people by the name of the cities or countries because I'm much too lazy to remember names.

Imagine I had a message here and I would expect you to understand what I say. Then I would be in trouble, I tell you. [Laughter] No. I don't take that risk. [Laughter] Many complain that last year I heard you say. They already play clever – I 'heard' you say. And maybe I even have said it. But the moment they say it, I have to destroy it like nothing. Then they say – but you said it. So what? Now it's bullshit. It was already bullshit when I said it. But you repeating it makes it more stinky.

Q [Another visitor]: Where Shiva starts, it ends...

K: Yeah. When Shiva pronounces Shiva, it already destroys Shiva. Because in pronouncing it, it destroys itself. The moment you pronounce yourself as a person, you destroy what-you-are. Even when Shiva pronounces itself as Shiva, it destroys itself. Imagine what happens when Shiva pronounces itself as Karl. [Laughter]

Q [Another visitor]: So, there's nothing to say?

K: Why?

Q: Because the moment you pronounce, it's destroyed...

K: Yeah because nothing is said by saying something. It's not as if there's nothing to say. There's saying without saying. They are empty words. So, I can talk for thousands and thousands of life times and I have never said anything. This paradox is permanent.

Q: And no one has heard anything?

K: And no one ever heard anything. Isn't it fantastic? No one ever understood anything. [Laughter] Isn't that wonderful? You don't have to compete with anyone because there was never anyone who understood anything. There's no competition in anything. But the moment there's one who understood something and one who understood a little bit less, the war of religion starts. Because understanding makes a religion, already – 'my' understanding. Then you have to compete and defend your bloody understanding. You want to make the understanding solid by repeating it to yourself a thousand times, just to get established in it.

Q: But competition happens...

K: Only when there's a competition of ownership, otherwise it's just a dance. But when there's competition, there's owner-shit. Then you compete in who is more shit or less shit.

Q [Another visitor]: How does this fit in to the 'absence of the tendency of avoidance'?

K: That's another bullshit. The person who made the DVD picked the title up from a different context and I don't correct anybody. It's like the books that come out, I never read one of them.

Q [Another visitor]: When they ask you in immigration about your purpose of visit, what do you say?

K: I am a tourist. I am everywhere a tourist, even in Germany. I am not lying, I never lie. [Laughter] You see that's good company because you are in the good company of liars. Everyone knows that everyone is lying. Even when you open your mouth you are lying and that is good company. You are in a company of lies. The liars are lies, whatever they are saying is lies and whatever can be said is a lie. This is a song of lies.

But the absence of a tendency of avoidance is not a bad pointer for what-you-are because what-you-are never had any tendency. So, you may call it the absolute absence of any presence or absence of any tendency. So, your nature is absolute absence or presence of any tendency or no-tendency of trying to avoid or not to avoid itself.

That's the *Mahabharata*. Yudhisthira could not avoid being what he was, there was no tendency left in anything. He ran out of the energy to avoid. By all the wars, by all the killings, by all what happened before, all the drama of the family, there was simply no energy left for avoidance. If this hell is for eternity, why not? May it be as it is. Then the whole hell, the whole heaven, everything is transcended into what-you-are. But it's not a doing; he could not do it one second before. It had to happen exactly as it happened.

Q [Another visitor]: I find this 'A-ha' confusing...

K: It's more than clear.

Q: But everyone is realizing...

K: Who is everybody? Who makes that oneness bullshit? I'm not sitting here and telling everyone that you are realized.

Q: You are realization…

K: No. You are not realization. You are Reality, if at all. But you will never realize yourself. So, it's not like everybody is realized. What an idea!

Q: I was always confused when I read that you have to be realized…

K: But who?

Q: I think you cannot not be realized…

K: Who?

Q: The phantom…

K: It's a part of realization but the part of realization cannot be realized. How can that be real? How can a phantom realize its true nature? When I say there was never any phantom who realized its true nature, I mean there was never anyone who was realized. What is confusing in that?

Q: I read in literature that you have to be realized…

K: Ah! In the literature, not here. You have to say that when you read books they claim to be realized and say that you have to realize. They woke up to their true nature and all of that. And how long have I been hammering here that all of that is a fake landing somewhere? And whoever claims anything, even having realized his true nature, can only be a liar. And you don't even have to worry; he will be punished by himself for that.

I know everything is confusing, the whole Bible is confusing, all the religions are confusing. All those confirm that you can do something. Even Buddhism is confusing because they say that by your good deeds, by your understanding, you can realize your Buddha-hood. But it all comes out of so-called phantoms creating a religion. Buddha would never have created Buddhism; he would have destroyed it right away. Christ would never have created

Christianity. He would not have been a Christian now. Buddha would not have been a Buddhist – for sure not.

It always needs Apostles, the ones who come later to make something out of what you say. Like now in Tiruvannamalai the Ramanaism has started. The Ramana religion is now full-on. There are so many disciples and so many teachers from that lineage, claiming that they are in the lineage of Nisargadatta, Ramana and all those famous guys. It's another religion – Advaita religion. I thought it was not possible to make a religion out of it. But they can do it, I am totally amazed. There are now even Advaita teachers! How can Advaita be taught? Imagine! How can one call himself an Advaita teacher? Non-duality teachers. Then they have non-duality conferences where non-duality teachers and scientists meet and talk about the ways of realizing your true nature. I'm fascinated!

So, I had to go and look at it. It's really not Advaita, it's Vedanta. None of them was Advaita. I thought I missed something but now I can be quiet again. [Laughter] I even thought I was arrogant not going there, but now I know that I'm okay.

Q [Another visitor]: What is the difference between Advaita and Vedanta?

K: They are two different directions. Normally it's Advaita-Vedanta. Advaita is Reality and Vedanta is realization of Reality. But now they turned it upside down. They make it Vedanta-Advaita. As if by Vedanta, you can reach Advaita. This is really a joke. It's always Advaita-Vedanta. Advaita is that what is without a second and Vedanta is the realization of it, the way it's realizing itself.

But now in that realization, there are masters and teachers that make it Vedanta and by Vedanta you can reach Advaita. How is that possible? But this is what happens these days.

Q [Another visitor]: So, Vedanta would be where you have meditation and stuff to do…

K: Yeah. Advaita is the Self – that which has no second. And by realizing itself, it is meditating about itself without any expectation or intention. Vedanta is meditation of Self about itself but not by expecting something to come out of it. But now they make it an expectation in Vedanta and the expectation is by meditation reaching your true nature.

You are already That what is Reality and you meditate as Vedanta about yourself. Meditation is action without intention. But now they make an intention into it, a meditator. And they say that you by your good meditation reach what-you-are. Then it becomes a joke.

Q: You cannot put the two together?

K: They cannot be together because they are not different in nature. Together means they are two. They cannot be together. There cannot be oneness of two. How can there be oneness of two? That's why I attack this bullshit – Aren't we all a bit realized bullshit. [Laughter]

Q [Another visitor]: You are almost mean...

K: I am mean, not almost – you know that. [Laughter] Nisargadatta was famous for that saying – meditation is action without intention. That's your natural state. The moment you realize yourself – the meditator, the meditating and what you meditate about, there's nothing to reach in it. You are already what-you-are but you still have to realize yourself in all the possible ways, in every possible meditation about yourself.

The next sip of coffee is the next meditation about yourself. But it doesn't make you more or less as you are. But Vedanta makes an idea out of it that by good meditation you become more as what-you-are.

Q [Another visitor joking]: Buy a good one...

K: Yeah. Become a good meditator and if you meditate ten hours a day, you become a better meditator and if you do TM then you are the Transcendental Meditator.

Q [Another visitor]: So all these ashrams are full of...

K: Greedy bastards! Club meditation. We have all the ex-customers sitting here. Don't get me wrong, I don't want to change it. I just want to point out; this is the way it is. This is not bad or good, it's just the way it is. And you believing in it makes you self-guilty – that's all. If you see it as it is, there's nothing to change in it. The world is as the world is and the world will always be business. Money makes the world go round and all the ashrams are made of money. If you go to Tirupati temple, there's mountain of money there and if you pay one thousand rupees you have two hours of less waiting. What is all of this? Making a nice wish and getting rich.

Q: Again, it is as it is...

K: I just make fun about it but I don't want to change it. Have fun, enjoy it. But don't expect anything out of it. It's neither fine nor bad or anything, it's just as it is. It's like a relationship with your mother, it will never be good. How can you have a good relationship with your mother who brought you into this bullshit life? [Laughter] You hate her from the beginning and for that you get more pocket money because she gave you this bad experience. Having a mother is hell. [Laughing]

If you could find anyone who loves to have a mother and would be fine to be alive. You will find no one who is fine to be alive. And if he's fine to be alive, he already hates that he has to die. So, there's no happiness in it. Crazy! Even when someone likes to be alive and enjoys it, he already hates it because he has to die. And a good relationship is the worst one. [Laughter] Because then you are afraid to lose it again. The bad ones are the best. [Laughter] Just have a bad relationship then you don't miss them when they are gone. [Laughter] It makes you happy!

It's same having the relationship with this body – the guy who wakes up in the morning – just hate it the moment it's there. And then you will be happy when it's gone and not ask what will happen to my poor body, my beloved, my precious. I invested so much organic food into it. [Laughter] All that plastic surgery, all for nothing. All the fat I was sucking out, all for nothing.

Actually I love it. I don't want to miss any of this joke. You cannot miss anything. As Absolute knowledge you are, in absolute stupidity you have to realize yourself. And if you look around yourself, even if you watch yourself, how stupid you behave – day by day. What you watch, what you believe in, where your ideas coming from and all of that, you don't need any other joke around you. [Laughter] You don't have to marry for that.

Q [Another visitor]: What makes you go to Tiruvannamalai after such a long time?

K: Maybe you can tell me. Do I have to know? That's what I like. I don't have to know why I do things. I don't have to book a hotel or a travel agent. I am a tourist and I already have a booked tour. I am totally booked out. This tour is booked totally. Every moment wherever I am, it's totally booked and I cannot make another journey. This is a journey that's already fixed – booked.

So, I don't have to know why I'm going to Tiruvannamalai, I just know it's booked – that's all. It's quite a peaceful travel. It's always wrong anyway, wherever you are its wrong.

Q [Another visitor]: You don't have to worry about changing tickets...

K: I cannot remember when was the last time I changed my ticket. I booked twice once because I forgot that I had booked. [Laughter]

Q [Another visitor]: What is faith?

K: Everyone fades away sooner or later, of that I have faith. [Laughter] I have the faith that I don't see anyone here again. [Laughter]

Q: As opposed to doubt...

K: Doubt and faith come together. Sometimes you have faith and sometimes you doubt. But then you even doubt your faith. The faith you can have, you have to doubt later.

Q: Is it just a belief?

K: Yeah. You believe that you have a faith. You have faith in your belief but you believe that you have a faith. Both come together. It's just a belief system and the belief system starts with the belief that you are somebody who needs faith. You left yourself, you be-leave, you become a leaf of the tree of life. Then you are not the tree, you are its leaf. Then you become a be-leaver. Then sooner or later, you be-leave that you become the tree again. No, the leaf has to fall. The leaf is just part of the tree but not the tree. It's not different from the tree, but it's not the tree. The moment the phantom is there, the phantom believes that the best the phantom can have is the faith in God or himself. But then it depends on it.

No. What-you-are never needs any faith and that what needs faith will fade away. It will fail and fail.

Q: So, what-you-are doesn't need faith?

K: It neither knows itself or anyone else. So, it cannot have faith in anything else because there are no two. There's not even one.

Q: The moment there is two, doubt comes in...

K: Even when there's one, there's doubt. When God knows himself, there's one God. And by being one God, he doubts himself. Then he has faith in himself. He meets two Gods, the God creating God having faith in God or himself. Crazy! Out of doubtful existence, he creates another doubtful existence of a doubtful God. Out of false, the false gets created. False, false, false.

No. What-you-are never needs anything – especially not faith.

Q: One should have faith in *Satguru*...

K: A good guru would destroy your faith. [Laughter] The moment you have faith in the guru, he has to do things so that you lose your faith. I like when Ramesh(Balsekar) had the scandal, all the fake disciples lost their fake faith. The ones who didn't care about what he was doing, they were just okay. It was okay anyway. But the ones who were with him because he behaved in a way that they liked him to behave, this had to happen. Existence made sure that this cannot continue. This falsity that someone has to live up to a standard, it will be broken.

I go even further. If Ramana would have had a girlfriend before the death experience, he would be maybe like Osho – you never know. He never said any word against sex or anything. There are incidents where he pointed at dogs and said that look what they are doing and you think you are doing something bad at night? They do it on streets and you think in the darkness you can do something bad? He had no moralistic or ethical stand-point, that's the sign of a *Satguru*. He never gave you any idea of faith or never asked anything from you. The one who asks you to have faith in him, wants to make you his believer.

No. You cannot trust anyone. No guru, no Self, no God, not even yourself – you know that. There's no trust needed and that's the beauty of it. The moment you exist and there's one who needs trust, it's already... No one will ever be trustful enough. It's a trust-fool – a fool of trust.

In India they invented the *Satguru* idea – the guru that had no idea about the guru or a disciple and has no stand-point of a good or a bad relationship and how a guru-disciple relationship should be. All of that are concepts. They just apply in Vedanta, where there is master and teacher and all of that. But a *Satguru* never gives you anything nor asks anything from you. There's no transmission.

The moment you have a discrimination of what you should do or shouldn't do, then he wants to sell fish. Then it stinks. He creates slavery. He wants to make you little – a slave of something. You have to behave like a slave, that's called religion. You have to behave in a certain way otherwise God doesn't love you.

Q: And you wouldn't get certain things...

K: Yeah. If you don't behave, you don't get anything. If you behave, you 'may' get something. There's a shepherd and you become a sheep, that's why you meh [Making sound of a sheep]. Then you become a slave – Master 'meh' I? 'Meh' you help me?

Papaji always said wake up and roar. He said you believe to be a sheep but actually your nature is a lion. But imagine you are a sheep and you wake up with lions. [Laughter] The last 'meh'.

Q: They say out of *vasanas* come desires and you must remove your *vasanas*...

K: Yeah and then you have to do karma yoga. Vipassana and all of that is trying to destroy your tendencies, sattvic living and all of that. Even Ramana gave advice but you have to know what the question was. There were people who came and said I cannot sleep at night or I get anxiety. Then he gave advice. If you want to sleep better, only eat sattvic. Don't eat garlic, don't eat onions. But out of that, giving an advice of daily life, they made a teaching of Ramana. If you want to get enlightened, don't eat garlic. [Laughter] Have you ever ate garlic-nun? [Laughter]

How many things you have to remember to have a sattvic mind. Don't eat this and that and it may even work. But the question always is – who needs that advantage? Who needs to have a peaceful mind? There's always one permanent answer – 'me'. And it will never be good enough. It will never be peaceful enough. The 'me' is a guarantee of misery. The 'me' lives by misery and not by a peaceful mind. So, it will make sure that even the most peaceful mind is not good enough. That's what 'me' is known for. It can doubt everything. And by doubting everything, even the most peaceful mind – it stays in misery.

So, the sufferer needs suffering. It makes sure that there would be suffering. The phantom needs all the phantom suffering to survive. Without suffering, there's no place for any phantom.

No 'me' without a discomfort. So, the 'me' makes sure that the discomfort continues. And discomfort is in doubt and faith and all of that. That is his realm, that is his playground and you cannot beat him in that. It's the beastly master of that hell.

That's why the 'me' is the devil and the master of the playground called hell. And you better be what-you-are inspite of it. You cannot beat him in his ground. You can only absolutely beat him by being what-you-are. So, let the mind fuck the mind and never-mind what the mind is doing or not.

Otherwise you are really in trouble and you have to really work your ass off – forever. Then you have to read Eckhart Tolle every day. [Laughter] It's painful. Then you have to listen to Oprah Winfrey. The new earth waits for you; you have to work for it. I think we should kill the entire humanity and save only the sperm of Eckhart Tolle and Byron Katie and Oprah Winfrey – the chosen ones. [Laughter] Then we make a new earth from it. It sounds more like hell again.

Who wants to be in that new earth? Let's keep this one; it's not good or bad. It's just bad enough for it.

Okay, that was Saturday night live from Mumbai. [Laughter]

February 9, 2013
Mumbai, India

Chapter Six

I Ask You To Be The Laziest Bastard You Can Be Because That's Your Nature

∼

Q: Yesterday you said that what-you-are is not the same as awareness…

K: Neither I am awareness nor am I not awareness. If I would say I am not awareness, I would still see myself as different from something.

Q: But that you are, that's awareness? I exist, I am aware…

K: That's not awareness. 'I Am' doesn't need to be aware to be 'I Am'. Now you can say because you are, there is awareness but you are not because there is awareness.

Q: But the sense that I exist…

K: It already needs one who is prior to that experience. The notion that 'you are' can only be there when you are already there before the notion 'you are' can be.

Q: That's true…

K: So, what are you? Are you the notion or That which is with and without the notion of 'I'?

Q: With and without...

K: So!

Q: But the sense that 'I Am' is there...

K: There is no notion in that in-no-sense of what-you-are. The notion is the beginning of a dream.

Q: The sense of existence is what you cannot not afford to be, is that what you are saying?

K: No. The sense of existence is a beginning of a dream existence. But that what is sensing the first notion, you can call it with and without sensation, with and without notion, you cannot not be.

Q: Is the sense of existence one of the seven states?

K: Yes. It's already a dream state.

Q: The impersonal awareness?

K: Even that's a dream state.

Q: You said awareness, I Amness and the world...

K: Those are the three personal states because it needs one who calls it awareness. When there's only awareness, awareness would not call itself awareness. You can call it as impersonal awareness. But only a personal awareness would call something as impersonal awareness. So, even that becomes personal. It needs a definer.

Q: The sense of existence doesn't need a definer...

K: But it's already a definition. That's the beginning of a definer, not even defining something. That's the first existence of 'I'. That's already the definer, from there you define. So, that's not your true nature.

Q: The sense of existence is already phantom?

K: You can say the realization of what-you-are starts with the sense of 'I' – the realizer realizing what can be realized. But the nature of the realizer is not the realizer. If you now define yourself as the dream realizer, it does not make you more stupid or less stupid than defining yourself as a body or being born. It's all part of ignorance. Wherever you land in that dream, you become a special definer landing on a special definition.

So, even if you define yourself as awareness, that sounds good – that's all. But it's as wrong as defining yourself as being a body or a person. Even defining yourself as being prior is still ignorance because what-you-are would never define itself as anything. It doesn't even know itself and then there is neither Self or no-Self. But the moment there is the self, the definer, then false starts.

[Door bell rings]

You see, the guest already comes too late. That's like you in the morning.

Q: But that is what you are, the sense of existence...

K: No. That's already a guest. It's already second-hand. You will never know yourself first-hand, in any relative sense. The knowledge has to be there, so that the knower can be sensed. So, the knowledge is sensing itself as a knower knowing what can be known. But it's not the knower not the knowing and not what can be known. It's very simple. To be what-you-are you don't need to know anything. To be what-you-are-not you have to know, you have to make an effort. Crazy!

So, I ask you to be the laziest bastard you can be because that's your nature – laziness. Why make all this effort? What would you say? Why do you make so much effort to know yourself? You only make an effort to know yourself because you already know yourself as something. Then you make an effort to know That, this doubtful I needs some security by having the knowledge of That.

Q: So, when Ramana said – just be...

K: He said be what-you-are, not just-be. You read something and then you repeat it in your own words. That's called trans-later. You can read all the books and most of them are 'later' – too-late. Someone translated with his understanding and wrote down what he understood. Then he even says 'Ramana said'. No, Ramana never said anything. They say something. It's their understanding. What to do? That's with all the books.

When I met Ranjit (Maharaj), he said don't read books of dead masters because there are not even living ones. There are only dead books, dead words... but today we launch one. [Laughter]

Q: You mean dead words but living persons?

K: There are no living persons. Where should they be? There are only dead persons. That's why I like books – because no one needs them, it's just for entertainment. If you make it to a teaching as if what I am doing is important for the world... mama-mia.

Q [Another visitor]: So, all his effort is useless?

K: He never put any effort. If existence wants you to do something, it gives you all the reasons and all the energy just to do what has to happen. So, don't claim that anyone has done anything – ever.

It's strange no moon days are warmer than full-moon days...

Q [Another visitor]: No moon resembles the black tantra...

K: Yeah. Shiva not knowing Shiva. That's why it's called Shiva moon, actually that's his natural state. Then tomorrow there will be a little awareness, the crescent moon. Then it already becomes a *jiva*-moon. The Shiva moon has absolutely no light and the first is already *jiva*-moon. Only one day a month there is Shiva, the rest is *jiva*.

Q [Another visitor]: The sense that 'I exist' comes later and 'I Am' exists before that?

K: It's not later, it's just that it's not always there.

Q: And the 'I Am' is prior?

K: 'I Am' is never-never. But the sense of awareness or the sense of 'I' is not always there.

Q: So, 'I Am' can be there without the sense of being?

K: That's called the deep-deep sleep.

Q: When Ramana says inquire – Who Am I?

K: It was always the wrong question.

Q: So, Ramana was wrong?

K: No. The translators always translated it wrong. His question was – 'Am I?' not 'Who Am I?'

Q: Without the 'who'?

K: Yeah. Without the ghost.

Q: It can be either 'What Am I' or 'Who Am I?'

K: No. Both are wrong. It's always – Am I. That's the meditation of 'Am I?' not 'Who Am I?'.

Q: Did anyone else say that or just you?

K: No. I was around the Ramana Ashram and read books from various disciples. Actually it doesn't matter who says it, I say it – that's enough. Everyone wants a famous name.

Q: So, you don't deny the 'I Am'…

K: I deny everything. [Laughter]

Q: Is there anything that you do not deny?

K: Even that I deny. I deny the denying.

Q: You are absolute nihilistic?

K: Not even that. [Laughter] Then I would leave something.

Q [Another visitor]: What is the difference between 'Who Am I?' and 'Am I'?

K: 'Who Am I' is a meditator question. 'Am I' is just meditation.

'Who Am I' is with an expectation of an answer and getting something out of it. 'Am I' is without expectation. One is a personal inquiry and the other is just 'Am I'. Who Am I always leaves someone who is prior, as a background. That's why the teachers and masters enter the prior state, like a canvas. That makes you someone. Then they say, I realized my true nature; being prior to the 'I'. But it's still a personal 'I' who is prior to that 'I'. It's still a person who makes a difference between the two.

Q: The 'I' is the ego?

K: Yeah. The ego that disappears in the background. Then that ego claims that he realized his true nature. Then I am real and everything else is not. That's the result of Who Am I, that's the problem. But 'Am I' you cannot make it personal. There is a silent answer, an unpronounced 'yes'. But it doesn't make you something what is prior. Am I leads to I Am, from the pronounced to the unpronounced which in nature is not different. Then there is no second, you don't become a reality which is different from something else.

Q: In 'Am I' the 'I' is still the ego...

K: In that 'Am I' the 'I Am' is the answer. In that, the ego cannot stay anymore. It cannot land anywhere. It can only land in the absolute 'I Am'. Then comes 'I Am That'. Finished. But from 'Who Am I', you can land up in the prior state.

Am I – I Am, that is what is nature of nature. It doesn't make anyone realized. The 'Who Am I' always creates someone who realized his so-called true nature. Then he becomes a realized master, an awakened one. He becomes established in something. But who needs to be established in something? That's the main question. And who then claims to be established?

I was happy when I read in one of Sadhu Om's books, where he pointed out that in Tamil, Ramana never said Who Am I, it was only Am I. Then there is a translator who says, it cannot only be 'Am I', there should be a question. As you said, Am I is not a question, it has to be a question, an inquiry and an inquiry needs an enquirer. 'Am I' is so natural, you don't even need to ask it but 'Who Am I' is a personal inquiry. Then it always expects an answer from it.

Q [Another visitor]: So, the follow-up of 'Am I' is 'I Am'?

K: It's an unpronounced I Am, that's your natural state. It leads directly to your natural state but not to someone who is the answer to the question. After a while it becomes Am I – I Am, a stream of That what-you-are. That's your nature. You are the presence but you don't experience any presence.

Q: With Who Am I, you can go back and back...

K: Yeah. You can go back to prior and different states. No. I am not feeding that.

Q: The little *jiva* keeps feeding on that...

K: Yeah. The little *jiva* survives.

Q [Another visitor]: So, even that is an ego state where there is realization or luminosity...

K: That's still a dream state. A *jñani* who enters a special state for sure is not a *jñani*. A *jñani* who still knows a *jñani*, is one *jñani* too many.

Q: Again there is a second...

K: There has to be one who landed somewhere. Reality that knows reality is for sure not reality. So, what to do? Whatever has a result which ends in something, for sure is a fleeting one. It's a temporary answer and then something else will happen. Who Am I is the inquiry and the result will be an answer. It would be a temporary one and it would be triggered by an inquiry. It's something new and what's something new, cannot be true.

But that you-are, no one has to tell you. It's not a special state.

Q: What is it to 'just be'?

K: 'Just be' would mean you are talking to someone. I am not talking to you. If I would tell you 'just be', it would be like an advantage for you. If you could manage just to be, it's like you have an advantage over someone else. That's why I would never say 'just be', I would say be what you are. But it doesn't mean you have an advantage by that. By being what you are, there can be whatever, mind-fuck or anything, whatever happens or not, no one cares. But 'just be' means you want to be someone without being bothered about anything. So, you are more quiet.

But I am not pointing to that. It's not 'just be'. Some manage it, they just be. But what kind of state is that, a demens state? One who is just without memory? What does it mean to 'just be'? No. The pointer is be what-you-are from Ramana but I always had people in America who would ask – How? So, in one talk I said – just be what you cannot not be. Then there's a gap, an absence, you cannot react to that. Later on you react to it. But for whatever time, there's an absence, a gap. It's like a koan you cannot break. But later on, for sure, you make it another concept.

No. If I tell you – be what you are, you immediately ask – How? How can I be what I Am? So, I make it a koan and tell you – be what you cannot not be. You cannot even follow it so fast.

Q [Another visitor]: Just be what-you-are is the same thing as saying just remain in what-is?

K: But for that you should know what-is. 'What-is' is what? [Laughter] It's still one too many, the one who is just what-is. It's still one too many. It will not stop you. You have to be what-you-are inspite of the ghost who inquires permanently and wants to know. This greedy bastard you cannot get rid of. But you try to create some understanding where he can rest? [Laughing] That's just a little pause, he gets energy out of it and then – Pang! Then he wants to tell others where they have to be as he just-is. [Mocking] Why are you not just being? I am just being. [Laughter] How can you not just be? Try to tell that to your wife or husband.

Out of all of that comes a teaching again, some result happens. Because 'just-be' is better than not just-be. It's amazing everyone wants to justify his existence and always wants to try a place where he can justify how he is and what he is. It always has to be very sound and stable so that no one can doubt you. You doubt yourself already enough, but you want to find a place where nobody else doubts you. Then you make a science out of it. What is that place where no one doubts? Just-be. Okay, I just am. You think no one will attack you there. When I want to be clever, I would just sit at home and watch television because no one will doubt what I say. [Laughter] But I am stupid enough to go into this fire. I don't claim that this talking is out of grace or out of compassion. This is out of stupidity, I tell you, as everything. [Laughter]

Q [Another visitor]: In 'just-be' there is still an element of time involved...

K: It's still time. Even no time is too much time because it's different to something else.

Q: Is being more relevant?

K: You can already compare being with non-being. So, it's already two. That's why *neti-neti* is more correct. You neither are nor you are not – neither-neither. The moment you claim that you-are and you just are, you already claim something because 'you are' and already that is too much.

Q [Another visitor]: It's the phantom raising its head again...

K: It has to justify his existence because it's a doubtful one. That's why this little phantom becomes a scientist, he really wants to know the truth. He claims that when I know who I am, I will be stable and sound. I wouldn't have to doubt myself anymore. But it will always doubt itself because every existence, being or not-being, is doubtful. Even not to be is doubtful. Being is doubtful, not being is doubtful because both are concepts. They are only there because there is one who pronounces being and experiencing. And who is this one who have to experience and not to experience himself?

Who needs to find a home where he can be as he is? Where I can be as I am, where I am accepted as I am, where I can rest for the rest of eternity.

I tell you, you can never rest. The phantom can never rest. And the rest it will find is temporary rest. Every night there is a temporary absence.

Q: And the phantom knows that it can never rest...

K: The phantom cannot know anything. How can something that is already known, know something? How can a knower who is known, know something? How can a dream object, dream or not?

Q [Another visitor]: Then why the hell does the stupid journey start?

K: You see, the 'why' again. Why not?

Q: There is no landing place...

K: But that's the fun. Imagine there would be a final landing place, that would be hell.

Q: There is no landing place...

K: There are many landing places but where you land, you have to depart again. Now you landed in this body and it will be gone one day. So, you have to depart. Then comes something else. [Laughter]

That's the fun of it. You are a business man, you want to get something out of it. And by that you suffer, you know that. And you should suffer, you would be punished just by being greedy and wanting to get out of it because greediness is painful. You always feel unsatisfied. You want more, greed, results – I want to land, I want peace, I want truth... me, me, me. That's the misery of permanent dissatisfaction. Then you get angry, you get jealous. That's exactly how you should be punished.

Q [Another visitor]: Sometimes there's a temporary satisfaction or comfort...

K: Not even that.

Q: In the relative...

K: Never-ever. There was never any satisfaction in anything. If there's a satisfaction that comes and goes and can be achieved by someone, then it's really a shitty one. You pay and go to a workshop and buy satisfaction?

Q [Another visitor]: To unlock your greed... [Laughter]

K: I thought in your case it was not necessary. [Laughter] That sounds good, unlock your greed... more and more and more. And what would be the result? To live your whole potential of greed. [Laughter] Some teachers say that I blow your ego so much that it will explode. [Laughing] Nice concept. Osho tried that and now look at them, all the Osho widows around. Super-egos, but nothing happened.

Q [Laughter: But he was going towards sexuality...

K: That is like blowing the ego, blowing the willy. [Laughter] Thank God it's all for fun. I have nothing against it but I tell you it's just for fun. I will never tell you don't do it, just do it. But it's not better than going to a shop and buying bread and butter. Going to a shop and buying and getting a little something is like a little success. Then you go to the next shop, a shopping mall, the next church, where you can get something for your bloody money. You really are looking for a compensation for all what you have done before. Going to workshops and getting something is not different than going shopping and it never worked for anybody.

Q [Another visitor]: Workshop works for sometime...

K: Before it works for one instant, you get more and more greedy. But it doesn't work. It makes you more and more depending and greedy for little orgasmic events. That's why America is full of churches – shopping malls.

Q [Another visitor]: So, whether you get junkie there or here...

K: It's cheaper here. [Laughter]

Q [Another visitor]: So, what is the difference between pleasure and desirelessness?

K: There is always pleasure and pain and you always swing between them. There is a thin line between them. Pain is the personal presence and the pleasure is the impersonal presence. Heaven and hell, pleasure and pain are always there. There is very thin line, you cross it very easily, you shift very easily between both of them and you cannot stay in one of them. It switches automatically, the whole day. Sometimes impersonal, pleasure; then personal again – pain. Discomfort, comfort, it's always like a flip-flop. They come together like a pair. I would say 50-50, 50% absence and 50% presence. That's the way it is.

But what 'me' wants to do is it wants to have 100% impersonal. That will never happen. I can just tell you, it always will be 50-50. If its 51-49, that person already calls himself happy or lucky. If it's 45-55, that's a seeker because it's unbearable. Then you are really in trouble, trying to find a way out because you are out of balance in that moment. If it's 50-50, you can just manage. If it's 40-60 then you already go to the mad-house because you cannot take it. The body gets sick, diseases happen. When you are stressed and more in personal thing, then the body reacts to that. But even that you cannot avoid. If there's supposed to be 80% pain, it will be there.

But in both ways, consciousness is the only experiencer experiencing itself in all of them and there always will be a balance. In one personal story, there may be more impersonal but for consciousness that's irrelevant. There are so many ways consciousness realizes itself, so many different camera positions, bodies to experience that in the end it's all balanced. There's as much pain and pleasure, darkness and light, good and bad. All of that comes as 50-50. As much darkness, as much light. As much goodness, as much badness, ugliness-beauty. All of that comes as a pair.

In that way you realize yourself because you can only realize yourself in two. There need to be differences. You cannot experience light when there is no darkness, you cannot experience darkness when there's only light. Bad can only be experienced because there is good, as an idea. And everyone has a different idea of what is good or bad. But all of that comes out of the goodness of what-you-are.

So, you are the goodness itself, the peace itself and you realize yourself in relative peace and relative war. But the origin of all of that, That what is realizing itself, is always peace. So, only peace is Reality, the peace of Absolute existence without a second because there cannot be any war. But That what is Absolute peace, That what is Absolute – without a second can only realize itself in differences, in difference of relative peace and relative war. And it will always be there, the world will always be peace and half will be war; or married and unmarried. [Laughter]

And that is the way you realize yourself. But for sure, the moment you try to get out of balance, if you want to have the impersonal side, then you are in trouble. Then you are out of your natural state because then you have preferences. And it seems to be natural that you have a preference of comfort. But for what-you-are, it's not natural. It's only natural for the unreal 'I' who has a preference of pleasure. Then you are in that pleasure and pain and you always fight against the pain for the pleasure. You become a warrior and you worry every moment about your pleasure, your comfort. That's called the care-taker, the personal care-taker who always tries to create pleasure or comfort. You only brush your teeth because you don't want to have the pain of the dentist.

Whatever you do is trying to avoid pain, trying to avoid something. Then you already try to avoid the future pain that may come by your not-caring. So, you become an insurance company within yourself. You try to do things now to insure that you don't have to worry later. You now eat good organic food because you don't want to be sick in the future. So, you are already sick because you don't want to be sick, in the future. That makes you sick now. Even the idea that you have to be healthy, is sickness, is a disease.

Q [Another visitor]: It's helplessness...

K: This is greediness. [Laughter] I want to smell good – that's greediness.

Q [Another visitor]: So, staying unmarried is also not the solution... [Laughter]

K: If you ask me, I like it more. But that's personal.

Q: I thought you would say, it's as bad as getting married...

K: No, no. For sure, getting married is the worst. [Laughter] You lose your balls instantly. Your balls are cut instantly by that ring on your finger. It's amazing. The moment you say – I will, the balls are gone. [Laughter] Then girls have a ball, but whose balls are they dancing with?

No, being a bachelor or married is too late anyway. Bible says take comfort in God, but who can do that? It's all too late.

Q [Another visitor]: Does it happen that it gets balanced?

K: No. In sleep maybe. But the moment you are awake, it's not balanced. Out of the unbalance, there will always be a tendency for something; an action comes out of the disharmony. There is no harmony in any moment. There is always a disharmony and that disharmony makes the whole universe move. That gives the beat to the universe. Not only you, the atoms, the molecules. If there would be harmony, there would be no movement possible, never-ever again. Like a clock, there's a disharmony to make it move.

Every moment has a little disharmony. Peace is never there. So, don't imagine that one day you would make it. But that's the joy of it. If there would be peace you can find, if there would be peace in any moment, then peace could be found. What kind of peace would that be? That peace could not be found, that's the joy of it. If you could find peace, you would be different from peace. Come on! If you could experience peace, you would be different from peace. Again, that would be two. If knowledge could be known, it would be a relative knowledge. If it could be owned by someone, what kind of bullshit knowledge would that be? And what kind of bullshit peace would it be which could be owned by someone or experienced? So, peace was never experienced by anyone. Never-ever.

But everyone is that, isn't it amazing? It's not an experience so it can never be lost and it cannot be gained by any experience. Isn't it wonderful? If you could gain it by any experience, it would be gained and you would fear to lose it again.

Q: So, the experience of happiness and bliss...

K: It's just a little less discomfort. No one ever experienced happiness or beauty. How can beauty be experienced? Where would it be? It would only be relative and relative is not beauty. That what is different from something else is not beauty. It's not just as ugly as the other one. [Laughter] So, beautiful women are amongst the ugly ducks not so ugly. Otherwise from what are all the make-up companies surviving from?

Q [Another visitor]: Standing in front of your painting...

K: My painting? They are ugly. Whoever claims to have a beautiful painting is a liar. There is no art you can experience. How can you experience art? You can only experience artificial experiences. They are artificial but they are not art. You can experience artificial life but never life. An artificial life depends on an experiencer, someone who defines what is not beautiful. It's all artificial. You can only experience concepts of different standpoints and reference points. But you cannot experience beauty or knowledge. Imagine if one claims to have experienced knowledge! What kind of knowledge would it be that you could experience? [Blowing in the wind] Junk.

Q [Another visitor]: Of course beauty is experienced by the phantom; you have art, classical music...

K: Keep dreaming. If two people go to the museum and look at the same painting, one is impressed and the other one says – I can do that myself. What bullshit! Where's beauty in that? It's just two different opinions. That cannot be art or beauty.

Q [Another visitor]: It's less discomfort...

K: It pleases your eyes and then you call it beauty. It just pleases your idea of how it has to be. Then you are pleased like a good customer because the business pleased you, it gave you some experiences that you expected to get.

Q [Another visitor]: That's the business of the phantom?

K: No. That's the business of museums [Laughter] and butchers and everyone is like a businessman. If you do a make-up, you please the visitors. So, you are a pleaser and you want to be pleased. That's your kind of... trying to control. And being loved, and getting attention because some people may pay attention to me. You 'pay' attention and you get paid, that someone looks at you and gives you recognition.

Q [Another visitor]: Is doubtlessness beauty?

K: I have no idea what is beauty.

Q: When I see you, I see doubtlessness...

K: That is my natural state.

Q: That's beauty?

K: I call it underwear. [Laughter] I don't have to call it anything. The moment you call it beauty, it's gone. The moment you call it Self, it's gone. The moment you call it anything it's already a concept. Because whatever you give a name, you make it different from something else. That cannot be it. When I say it's an absolute absence of any presence of any idea or no-idea of what-you-are and what-you-are-not, I have to make it complicated. That's maybe a pointer to what-you-are, the absolute absence of any presence of any kind of one who knows or doesn't know what he is and what he is not. That's maybe a pointer to what-you-are; to that what is knowledge which is absolute independent of anyone who knows or doesn't know anything; or absence. Neither depending on the presence or the absence of anyone who knows or doesn't know what one is.

That's your natural state or your nature which doesn't need to know nature to be nature. And that what needs to know nature, is already too late. That's called the phantom. The depending phantom who always tries to define what is Self or nature or art and will never succeed. It will always be different; never ending story of consciousness trying to define consciousness. It's an infinite scientist who tries by all means to find its nature; never ending story. Every year they have a different conclusion, going deeper, going higher, different way of looking at it; never ending story.

That's your dream. Your dream affair, your dream business and your dream connection. Then you want to unify yourself again with what you are, always a nice idea. I only want to experience oneness with myself. This preference, that's suffering. That's the basic suffering of a good intention – to know yourself. Everyone says I just want to know myself. I don't deny any good intention; all intentions are good because they come out of the goodness itself. The goodness wakes up to awareness and from there everything begins.

The *Parabrahman* was already there before he knows himself as Brahman. Brahma is not born in experiencing itself. So, as nothing is born in the first place, nothing gets out of that. Everything is already there. So, nothing ever happened in the purest awakening of *Parabrahman* waking up to awareness. It starts to become aware to exist. In that nothing happened because its nature was already there, without awareness. So, nothing happens in the beginning. And if nothing happens in the beginning, whatever comes from that, nothing happens.

So, nothing is done from that point. He was not lost in awareness and he cannot be gained again. Nothing ever happened. So, be what-you-cannot-not-be means be That. And that is satisfaction by nature because there is no one who needs to be satisfied – never needed to be satisfied. But the rest cannot make you satisfied – Thank God and praise the Lord!

The rest is merely the dream of a businessman who has nothing to offer. Empty shop!

Q [Another visitor]: In awareness, did something happen?

K: No. In that first happening, nothing happens.

Q: Can you explain what do you mean by that?

K: The meaning is that the Absolute *Parabrahman* is not affected by being aware of its existence.

Q: That's why you say nothing happened?

K: That's why I say nothing happened in that happening because nothing is created.

Q: The creation is not affecting it but the creation is there...

K: The creation is the result of the *Parabrahman* waking up. But even the creator is a part of creation. Who created the creator? Because that what is creating the creator, was, is and always will be – what-is. So, the creator never created anything.

Q: Nature created the creator...

K: There is no creator of the creator. Then there would be two.

Q: Creator created awareness...

K: How can he create awareness? You create two again. You make one as awareness and other one as origin of awareness.

Q: When awareness is, it's already too late...

K: By the experience of two, there are no two. As in the beginning there are no two, there is no problem in the beginning and there is no problem at the end. There were never two but still you experience two.

Q: Then why do you say it's too late?

K: Whatever is done after that, all the sensational experiences is too late or too early – whatever you like. Nothing ever worked for anyone, never needed to work.

Q: Too late implies time...

K: When there is experience, there is time and when there is time, it's too late or too early. But it's never right.

Q: Ramana gives an analogy of screen and projections on that screen. How good is that analogy?

K: If it helps you, it's good otherwise it's bad. [Laughter] You have to decide it yourself. For one, it stops him and for other one it just makes another concept. You can never know. I say so many things, for someone it's a total yes and for the other it's the opposite. You never know. That's why there's no universal key, one sentence that fits everyone. There are so many keys and so many doors and everyone seems to have a different door which has a different key that stops him. I have no idea. I talk so much and I give so many keys, I really don't know which is the right one. I just use every key, whatever comes out. Then maybe by accident, if it's meant to happen, the key fits. Then when the key fits, everything is like an absolute yes. How could I ever believe in anything else?

Nisargadatta and Ramana talked so much without a filter, not asking anyone what was their understanding, just hammering. Then one of the things makes the puzzle complete. When the puzzle is complete, you are complete and by your being complete there was never any 'me'. How can there be any 'me' when there is the completeness of what-you-are – your natural state. You can never know which word will be the last for the puzzle. The one that fits and the puzzler is gone because he has nothing to do anymore, he is out of business. Totally out of business in one split second.

Q: So, there is something like the last puzzle?

K: The last puzzle is always the puzzler. The puzzler always missing himself in the puzzle. By your intention to make the puzzle complete, you get out of the puzzle. You want to see the puzzle; you want to experience the puzzle. And by that, you are puzzled because there's always something missing – Shit! Whatever I do is never in harmony because there's always one asshole missing. Who is that guy? Then maybe with the Am I, you automatically go into the puzzle. You cannot stay outside. Am I – I Am, suddenly the puzzle is complete. You have an experience of completeness, instantly. Just by Am I – I Am, there's a completeness of what-you-are. That I could not find in Who Am I because there's always like a puzzler who went through the puzzle, behind the puzzle. Then he's still puzzled or beyond the puzzle or under the puzzle or is aware of the puzzle.

So, Am I – I Am is an instant completeness. It seems like a peace you cannot deny. You have to make an effort to get out of it again. You have to make a little effort to get out of it and try to puzzle again. That's why Nisargadatta said, 24 X 7: Am I – I Am. And you don't need to specially sit down or do anything special. It's just moment by moment staying in the Am I – I Am. By that, naturally the puzzler gets erased, he has no place anymore.

But again, if it's meant to happen it will happen. If not, you will be puzzled even by that. [Laughter] Otherwise it sounds like a recipe again. Then as a puzzler you want to get one with the puzzle. But by trying to be one with the puzzle, you still remain as a special person trying to be one with the puzzle. Then you are the oneness puzzler. [Laughter] It's crazy! Then suddenly he claims that I am one with everything. But who is in oneness with what? So, he's still a special puzzler who is one with everything. It's so dangerous and the tricks are so infinite. Crazy, crazy! But what to do?

Q: You say if it's meant to happen. So, there's a cause and effect?

K: No. You start the movie business, you are guilty. The movie is already shot and if one of the frames of the movie is such that the puzzler is one with the puzzle, it's already there in the movie. So, if the future frame implies that you as a puzzler gets one with the puzzle, it has to happen – has already happened. So, it's not a cause and effect, it has already happened. There is no cause for it. It's just one aspect of realization which has already happened.

Q: It's not clear to me...

K: If it would be clear for you, you would not be here anymore. [Laughter]

Q: But I am here...

K: Because you are here, you are not here-now; you are here-later. As before and later you are here and not as here-now. When you would be here-now, there would be no 'you' sitting here. There would be no puzzler and there would be no puzzle. But as you are here before and after, you are puzzled by that what happens now. You want an after-effect, that's what you are here for. I want to have something from my understanding; I want to have something from me being the puzzle. How can I get something out of being the puzzle? You still want to get something from it. You want to have an advantage of being the puzzle.

But there will never be any advantage of being the puzzle. Or you can say it's the absolute advantage of being the puzzle because it doesn't need any advantage. The one who needs an advantage by being one with the puzzle; he would still be puzzled by that. He still remains as a puzzler – a realized puzzler.

Q: But what do you mean by – if it's meant to happen?

K: If it's meant to happen means it has already happened. If it's in the movie and it's meant to happen means it will happen in spite of what you do or don't. You cannot postpone it and you cannot make it earlier. That's what it means by – if it's meant to happen it will happen. Not because of what you do or don't do.

Q: Who has produced the movie?

K: It was never produced, that's the problem. The realization and Reality are never created. There was never any creation. Nothing ever happened means the realization of the total block of manifestation of whatever is in existence, is for now and forever. It never came, it will never go. You think in timeframes. That something was created and now where did it come from? You are puzzled by all those things. But if it's a total block of existence, nothing ever comes and nothing ever goes, nothing is ever created, where is your puzzle? There's silence. It's not a silence which is prior to something. It's not a silence which is coming or going. It's the silence of existence. This what is right-now here-now. This is silence of existence. This moment in its nature is infinite, never created, never goes. Nothing is ever born. Not even the one who claims that 'I am the unborn'. [Mocking] Everything else is born, but I am the unborn. [Laughter] That's the little difference.

This is never born. Whatever-is is never born. So, it cannot die, there's no death. No birth no death in anything. Life is never born and life will never die in anything; and this is life. So, where is birth and where is death? Only a dream. The question where it comes from is only in the dream.

Q [Another visitor]: So, this moment is perfect?

K: It's neither perfect nor imperfect. It doesn't mean anything. [Laughter] Forget perfection. That's the beauty of existence; it never needs to be perfect to be what-it-is. And that what needs to be perfect, for sure is a dream of life. It can be absolutely imperfect and it still is the absolute. What bullshit life needs to be perfect? Only a relative one. It never loses its nature by being perfect – gaining something or being imperfect – losing something. But it cannot be other than Absolute. Absolute means there is no second edition of it. There is no second edition of existence at all. There's not even a first one. And when there's not even the first one, what is there to compare?

If you make it one, you compare it with that what needs two. But if there's not even one, there's neither comparing nor not comparing. Then you are really out of business. You close down your shop. But it was never open in the first place. [Laughter] That's the whole problem, you never had a shop and it never opened. And now you want to close it down. You become a whole seller – I give up everything, I devote everything just to be what I Am. And I give everything I don't have. Especially that what I never had, I freely give. I just be and I let be. Now we are coming to that bloody 'just be'.

Q [Another visitor]: I had an experience yesterday that I am fed up…

K: Welcome to the club. I was fed up even before I started to talk. You needed that I talk to you; I didn't have to listen to myself. But you are right, there's no advantage of listening to this. This is meditation.

Q: I am fed up but I still like to be in your presence…

K: That's a paradox. There are many like that. They say they hate that they have to be with me. But this is meditation, something happens in spite of you liking it or not. But it was always the case. No one asked you to be born. The circumstance always dictates. And for me it's always like a rape. Then for me it's like there is a rape but it doesn't mind to be raped by himself. That's all. I really don't mind to be raped by what I Am. And I can blame myself forever but it will not make any difference. I would rape myself again and again. And I am the Absolute rapist, the rape and what is getting raped – moment-by-moment I experience myself. Total helplessness! Absolute impotent to change any single dot of the dream or the realization.

In spite of being the almighty Absolute, no way of changing what-is. That I like in the *Mahabharata* when Krishna says – In spite of being the creator, being the blue-print of all possibilities, I cannot change one little aspect of it. But that's the nature of when there's no second. There's no possibility of any control. You cannot control anything as there are no two. You are the energy itself but the energy itself has no energy. So, there's nothing to do with it.

Q: It doesn't make sense…

K: But that's the beauty of it. It doesn't need to make sense. Doesn't make sense means I cannot work it. And I am not here to give you tools of control. Actually, I try the opposite. I try to take all the tools away, the belief that you have a tool, that you have a recipe. I am here to destroy those ideas. That's why I say this is not a school or a teaching. If it were, you could have become a master or had a diploma or a degree which you can work with and make money with it and get something out of it. This is the total opposite.

Q: And yet the fear of being destroyed comes...

K: Yeah that will continue forever. That's the way you realize or experience yourself; always in fear. Fear cannot be destroyed. How can you destroy false evidence? A non-existent dream of time. How can you kill time? There was never any time, that's the whole problem. How can you get rid of something what was never there? How can you kill an illusion when there was never any illusion? When all there is, is life or Self, how can you destroy the absolute existence? This is absolute existence. How can you get rid of what-you-are? How can you leave what you are?

I can just say every attempt is painful and suffering. But even that you cannot stop. You are fucked forever. [Laughter]

Q [Another visitor]: It's not a rave party; it's a rape party... [Laughter]

K: I can only say that I am not here to bullshit myself in anyway. And I am absolutely unable to create hope. Maybe I can try [Laughter] but it doesn't work. Immediately everyone starts laughing. They don't buy it from me.

Q [Another visitor]: You create the most exquisite hope... [Laughter]

K: Now we want to know how and what kind of hope.

Q: I don't know... [Laughter]

Q [Another visitor]: Can you talk about the natural state...

K: Ramana talked a lot about it.

Q: Is it the state that are in without trying to be other than what-you-are...

K: The natural state is the state in which you don't know anymore what is natural and what is not natural. The total absence of one who knows of what is and what is not natural. That would be your natural state.

Q: Is it the state where you one is not trying to be what one is?

K: No. That would be a special state again. In that natural state, no one can be. In the natural state, only nature is. Now life is here – this is nature. If there would be space-like spirit, then that would be nature. If there would be awareness, then awareness would be the nature. If there would be the absence, then the absence would be the nature. So, you don't know what-is and what-is-not nature anymore because you are nature.

Q: Suppose I want to know 'my' natural state...

K: That's already one too many. It cannot be your natural state.

Q: I cannot be in my natural state?

K: No. There is no inside and no outside.

Q: Just being is not enough?

K: No. Just being is still 'you' just being. It can never be owned and never be reached by anyone. It's just that what you cannot not be. This is what no one will ever attain – unattainable, unreachable – that's what you are. That's your nature. But trying to reach it, trying to attain it that makes you a phantom. So, you never left the natural state.

Q: The natural state is...

K: It's just your Absolute nature – just being the Absolute. The Absolute not even knowing the Absolute, of what is Absolute and what is not. That what is without a second, without any idea of what-it-is and what-it-is-not. The main problem is that you never left that state. You never left your nature. By now trying to attain it again, you imagine to be out of it. So, it's an imaginary outsider who wants to go back. But by whatever he tries, he cannot go back. He can only reach some relative states, but can never reach where he is not.

Q: Is he better-off by not trying to go back?

K: Only in the dream there are people who are better-off and not so well-off. But for what-you-are, there's neither good nor bad.

Q: I'm just asking if it's better-off...

K: In the natural state there's no one who is better-off. It has no attribute. It is just that what is the Absolute. That what is Self not knowing Self. That what is Brahman not knowing Brahman. Not knowing what-is and what-is-not Brahman – that's your state. But any moment you define it, you are out of it. Then it becomes artificial. Knowledge doesn't need to know anything. So, Knowledge is your natural state – being Knowledge. The Knowledge doesn't allow any knower.

When you are what-you-are, there is knowledge, but there is no knower. When there's a knower, there's no knowledge. Both cannot co-exist. When there's truth, there's truth. But when there's one who knows truth, there's neither.

Q: The one who is in the natural state will not know he's in the natural state?

K: No. There's no 'one' in natural state. In nature, there's no one. No one ever attained, as no one was ever there so no one could ever get out. That's another problem. There was never anyone in natural state, so never anyone could get out of his natural state. There was never any one or no-one in That what-you-are. Now you dream yourself as one. That's the dream story. You dream a dreamer, you dream the dreaming, you dream what can be dreamt. But the dreamer is already dreamt by the Absolute dreamer you are. But in the Absolute dreamer, you cannot find any dreamer.

Parabrahman is neither personal nor impersonal. It experiences itself as personal or impersonal. But it's neither personal nor impersonal.

Q: Is there any distinction between *Parabrahman* and the natural state?

K: To be what is *Parabrahman*, would be your natural state. In nature, there's no difference in nature.

Q: So, it's just another name for natural state?

K: Yeah. Just two names for it. Your Absolute nature or *Parabrahman* in nature are not different. They are not two. And no one can enter there and no one can attain that and no one left it. As I said, there was no one in the beginning. There is no Brahman in *Parabrahman*; there are no two natures from the beginning. Only if there were two natures, one nature could get out of nature.

Q: When the dream ends, is the natural state attained?

K: The dream will never end. That's the problem.

Q: 'If' it ends?

K: It will not. It's a dream that the dream can end. It's a nightmare that you hope that the dream may end. This never ending dream, never starting – it's just a dream. The nightmare starts when you think it may end one day. Then it becomes a nightmare because you have to be ready for that. What will happen then? Then you doubt. Am I ready for that? Will I be in the right mood when that happens? [Laughter] So, you meditate to be in the right mood, just for the dream to end. Om... Om... Om... 24 X 7. [Laughter]

Q: Just as no one was responsible for starting the dream, it will come to end one day...

K: No. It cannot come to an end. It never started, that's the problem. It's a dream that there was a beginning. It's a scientist's dream of a big bang. The big bang never happened. God became a scientist and then be dreamt about a big bang. [Laughter] Now he wants to be banged. You can wait a long time. Every year they have a different theory.

Some scientists became Buddhists others became nihilistic, denying everything and all of that are merely concepts anyway. Destroying everything is a concept and the opposite too. No one will ever know what one is and what one is not. The Truth which can be spoken, for sure is not the truth. Truth is never beautiful and beauty is never true. That's the first premise in Tao.

And I agree truth is never beautiful. If I tell you this will never end, hell will always be there for you, doesn't sound so beautiful. You will never make it; you will always be a leftover. [Laughter] You are the absolute leftover. Everything may go or come but you still will be what-you-are inspite of coming and going and all ideas, you are That. And you have to realize yourself in heaven and hell. That's the consequence of you being what-you-are, Reality itself, you have to realize yourself infinitely – in whatever possible way. It will always be in pairs – of good and bad, of pleasure and pain, of comfort and discomfort. If you like or not? Are you ready for that? Can you take that?

Q [Another visitor]: [Joking] Give us one day to think about it... [Laughter]

Q [Another visitor]: When you ask – Can you take that, do we have any choice?

K: There's neither one who has or has-not.

Q: Can you give us some hope?

K: I have nothing against hope but it wouldn't make any difference. [Laughter] That's the last hope that you hope that I don't give you any hope. But do you really think I would care about giving or not giving hope? I can give you hope. [Laughter]

If I would make a teaching that hope is bad and you should not have hope, I would not care. Hope or no hope what would be the difference? As the scientist would say, there is a difference. But would it make a difference for what-you-are? Can it make you different? Or your nature?

In that sense by all those happenings, nothing ever happened.

February 10, 2013
Mumbai, India

Chapter Seven

The Experience Of Silence Is Not Silence

~

Q: Maharaj says unless you see the tremendous sorrow of your life and revolt against it, a way out cannot be found...

K: Your idea is that you can get out of the sorrow; there can be an evolution of your spirit, an evolution of your consciousness. You always want to have something more, something to grow – growing spirit, growing of your spiritual life. Becoming an advanced seeker, succeeding in something. You will always fail, that's the pointer. Then there's a revolution. Out of an evolution, comes a revolution. Revolution means you chop whatever can be chopped; you kill all concepts by being what-you-are.

But as long as there is a little hope for your future evolution, that you may get it in some whatever future by going into a deeper state of peace. Maharaj used to say I only talk to people who have turned around.

Q: What does he mean by a way out cannot be found unless you revolt...

K: You still see that there is a possibility to reach your goal outside.

Until you see the emptiness of all goals and emptiness of all concepts, the spirit turns within, turns around. Then there's a revolution and then there's no way out. Sooner or later, you will be gone.

Q: Even when it turns within, there's no way out?

K: There's no way out because you would be dropped sooner or later anyway. But that's the revolution; when the self only gives attention to the Self and not to any relative concept anymore of future happiness. When you see all the happiness as fleeting and all the knowledge you can gain as empty, all of that doesn't satisfy you in the slightest possible way, then there's a revolution. Ramana called it as the spirit turns to itself. The Self turns to the image of what the Self is.

Then there's no way out as well, sooner or later it will drop you if you like it or not – as a relative idea. And without that nothing will happen anyway. In that sense, I am happy that I only talk to the left overs who are really fed up and really have no hope in anything. All these hopeless cases sitting around me. For me it's actually good. I rather don't talk to the crowd that has hopes because then I can only make fun. I am too lazy for that.

Q: When there are so many human beings, plants...

K: If there would be one human being that would be quite something. Just show me one and prove that there's a human being.

Q: I cannot...

K: No one can. You cannot even prove that there's energy. The scientists are trying to find matter but they are not able to find the matter. Where are the humans? If there would be a reality of humans, then they should not be born or die because whatever is born and dies cannot be real. It's a temporary experience of humanity, but it cannot be real. What kind of humanity would it be which is temporary and comes and goes and is fleeting?

Humans are just an idea. Consciousness just has a mask of humanity. It wears a mask called human; there are seven billion masks now. But the reality of all of that is consciousness. Consciousness plays the role of humanity. So, what is real – humanity or consciousness?

Q: Consciousness...

K: It seems like. Normally humans claim that they have consciousness, 'my consciousness'. It's exactly the opposite. Consciousness owns humanity, consciousness owns the owner. Then the owner claims that he has an evolution.

Q: With the seven billion beings, how is it that there is a continuous sense of evolution and involution?

K: It's like your body. You start from zero, then you grow and at one point there's a revolution. By that you go down to your grave. So, it comes up, appears and disappears. The appearance of something is an evolutionary appearance. The revolution is like a disappearance. Evolutionary appearance and revolutionary disappearance.

Q: Why do so less numbers of people become hopeless cases?

K: They are all hopeless cases, they just sit in the bar and do the bar meditation or go to football. You think there's more hope in football? Or having a drink every night? Or having a wife that shouts at you? [Laughter] They are all hopeless cases but there's still a tendency of evolution. If you become an alcoholic or a drug junkie, it's already like a revolution because you gave up hope. You already try to commit suicide.

So, there's a tendency of life going out, embracing and doing things, an evolution of life. And the revolution is the tendency of suicide. A meditation is intentional suicide. You want to avoid something; you want to go back where you belong. You had enough of being a human, you had enough of having a form, then you meditate on spirit. You want to be space-like spirit, you want to kill your body, you want to get rid of something. It's like killing something.

But first you are full of – I will make a woman happy forever, like a warrior. Then when he's fourteen there's the first shock and on twenty eight there's another shock. If you ask people when you went to Osho, it will mostly be twenty eight or fifty eight. Now everyone is counting their age. [Laughter] Immediately they jerk with themselves. Even in astrology they have fifty eight as the second ego return. Many people die at fifty nine because they are fed up for the second time.

Q: Omar Khayyam says How come man has not become depressed enough in this pointless life. Everyone seems to be running around...

K: Everyone has families to run, things to do. Ramesh would ask – do you have enough money to sit here and seek. If you are on the street and have no money, you would have no time to think about yourself. It's already a luxury that you think about Self, that you have a depression about yourself. [Laughter] You have enough spare time to get depressed.

Q [Another visitor]: Luxury tax...

K: I think it's normal that not so many are interested in this. Normally everyone is much more business-like. They would go for paintings and hobbies, whatever pays them, whatever pays them – relaxation or peace. They can show it to their family; they can show it to their friends. It's more for the social network. This is not for social network. For this, you have to be more alone. This puts you in solitude.

Normally, as long as it's possible to go astray and play around, you will do that. If you cannot do that anymore, then you face your solitude. That's not by choice, no one makes that choice. The normal tendency is a social life, having parties, work, family and all of that. So, it's already like a recall, like a car that really doesn't run. Normally out of hundred thousand cars, ninety nine thousand five hundred cars run well. But then there are a few cars which are really not well done. [Laughter] That's called a recall for final maintenance.

Q [Another visitor]: All the spare parts are gone...

K: It has run out of fashion.

Q [Another visitor]: Thank you for so much hope...

K: Hopeless cases. You try to justify why you are here. Everyone wants to fight and tries to know why.

Q [Another visitor]: Maharaj would say if at all you want me to prescribe something, I would say be earnest...

K: No. That's in I Am That and we already talked about it last year that it has a totally different meaning. Instead of earnestness it means in Marathi that if totality decides to do it, you will do it. It doesn't depend on your earnestness, it's upside down. If they say that you have to be earnest, then for sure it was wrong.

Q [Another visitor]: Is it a description?

K: They just translated it wrong.

Q [Another visitor]: I Am That was totally different from other books...

K: Yeah. Because it was from a translator who was totally not familiar with the language. He always had to fit things together.

Q: But Maharaj often called Maurice Frydman as a *jñani*...

K: Because he claimed to know. He was making a joke about him but he took it seriously. You can never know, I was not there. I think Jean Dunn was more accurate. You are right, when I read I Am That, I would say no to every second thing. But what to do? Later on Maharaj said, forget the whole book. But he's famous for that book. If only other books would have come out without I Am That, he would not have been so well-known. So, it has a purpose, you never know. It's like a teaser, like an appetizer. Because the food you may not like it later. [Laughter] You have to be tricked into it. Existence is so tricky, I tell you. I don't say it's wrong, it's just an introduction.

Q: Is the concept of the pain body same as *vasanas*...

K: That's Eckhart's idea. You can book him for four hundred dollars on internet and ask him.

Q: I don't need the answer... [Laughter]

Q [Another visitor]: If this is an eternal moment, does it mean that the phantom keeps returning to this moment?

K: No. The Self will always experience itself as this moment, again and again. There was never any phantom experiencing anything. The phantom is an experience which is part of this moment. But the Self will always experience the experiencer the experiencing what can be experienced in this moment again and again. You think you as the phantom have to come back and experience it again. The Self would be here again and will have to experience it again and has no memory of it. So, there's no problem with it. But for you, it will be again and again and again.

Q: So, when you say we have had this conversation before...

K: The Self experienced this moment infinite times before. There's no 'we' involved in that. This conversation, this infinite now, never came and will never go and you will always have to experience it in the loop of infinite realization of what-you-are. This frame of the movie will always be experienced again and again. The Self is the Absolute witness of whatever-is and whatever-is is the infinite.

Q: The Self cannot experience this conversation?

K: The Self has no conversation; the Self is experiencing a conversation. The Self is dreaming this moment as a conversation but the Self does not have any conversation. There is no someone who has something. The Self will realize itself as this moment again and again.

Q: This moment as in now?

K: This, exactly as it is now, it never came and it will never go. There is no again. This experience is as infinite as this experience

– never born, never dies. Nothing is ever created and nothing will ever die. So, if nothing is ever created, this moment is not created and this moment cannot die. If this moment could die, it would be separate from existence. How can that be?

In a dream everything can happen, but only in a dream. What to do? But that's called silence. It's not a silence which is somewhere behind you, this is the silence you experience. Silence means no coming, no going. There was never any time in anything because time means coming and going. There is no birth, there is no death. This moment is never born and it can never die; never created, can never be destroyed.

That's the nature of this moment – infinite. It's not like one is not born and one cannot die; one who claims that he is not born and everything that is born and dies is not real. This 'one' again is one who makes himself as special to something else. This is what-you-are – right now. You are the seer, the seen, what can be seen in total. You are the witness, the witnessing, what can be witnessed, in this infinite now. The nature of you – the witness, the nature of witnessing and the nature of what is witnessed is not different. So, life living itself is that very experience. And there's nothing born and nothing dies in that – including that what is again and again.

Q [Another visitor]: My wife says that I always do things wrong...

K: That's the nature of man. I have to admit she is right. Whatever men are doing is wrong because they don't do anything. You never listened to your wife, you never did anything right. And I am happy about it that I cannot do anything right. That's peace. If you cannot do anything right, you cannot do anything wrong. Both come together. If you can do something right, then you can do something wrong. But if everything is wrong, [laughing] I am fine.

I always point to that what cannot be taken by anyone. If you want to take it as a relative one who tries to understand it, it makes you depressed. I like that. If you really want to understand it and put it in your pocket and own that understanding, it makes you depressed. Even by understanding that, you become depressed by it. Because you think again and again, there's no way out, poor me. An infinite self-pity comes, even by that understanding. It's crazy.

But for what-you-are, it's still unaffected. But the phantom who understands that, in that understanding you get depressed. That's called the dark night of the soul. No way out, again and again. So, when you are this relative one, it's impossible to bear. You cannot take it. When you are what-you-are, there's nothing to take. Absolutely fine. This absolute, who cares? If this is for infinite, for eternity, who cares?

But if you look at it from the relative [whining] This pain again, all over again [crying mockingly]. So, you better be what-you-cannot-not-be because there is no problem. It doesn't need to understand that.

Q: Heisenberg said you cannot know the speed and position of the particle at the same time, so you will never know something exactly...

K: You will never know truth, you can only guess. It's only there because you observe it and if you don't observe it, it's gone.

Q: Your observation influences it...

K: You created it by observing it. If there is no observer, there's nothing to observe.

Q: If I want to know something, even while I am wanting the thing has changed...

K: You create what you want to know by your wanting it.

Q: And it changed while I wanted to know...

K: But you create the scientist who wants to find that answer, he will create that answer.

Q: My wanting is already an influence?

K: It's not an influence. You are looking for something and by your looking for something; you will find it and not the opposite. From a relative stand-point, even the one who wants to understand has the pressure to understand and it will put him down low and depressed. So, even that understanding doesn't give him freedom. It's still a misunderstanding. No way out.

But for what-you-are, which is the understanding itself, neither knowing nor not knowing itself, there was never any problem. This little understanding or big understanding, whatever that means, is still a load for that phantom. It will not make a difference. But why not put some more load on the shoulders of the one who wants to carry?

Q [Another visitor]: The observer and the observed come together?

K: They come together and disappear together.

Q: Can we say the same thing for the creator as well?

K: Yes. The seer, seen and what can be seen come together.

Q: Some teachers say there is a seeing but no seer...

K: That's an old esoteric thing. Knowing without a knower, seeing without a seer. You can dump that. [Laughter] Who makes the difference when there's a presence and an absence of a seer? For who is there only seeing? It's like catching a fish; you create a little hook with a worm. That's like seeing or knowing. Then you give your intention to that little hook and you are hooked on that little worm. Because you think – just being is better than the one who is living.

It's like oneness is better than separation. But in knowing there's no separation, there's just knowing. There's only experiencing but neither experiencer nor what is experienced. So they make something better than other one. And maybe there's an advantage. But the one who needs an advantage is a relative phantom. It can only be a phantom advantage. So, the relative advantage of dream is the relative advantage of the dream. When there's only dreaming without a dreamer and what is dreamt, that would be the power of now because there's only knowing. There's no past, no future in it because there's no knower. There's no one who makes a story out of that knowledge. It seems it's more comfortable. But who needs that comfort?

So, it's the power of now that makes you more comfortable because there's no pain body in it. The pain body exists only when there's one who has the experience of the body. So, he wants to end pain, the suffering. But who needs to end the suffering? Always the same question – Who needs it? And who has an advantage of something to end. There needs to be a hidden phantom who needs an advantage. Even that advantage in that nature is disadvantage because there's one who needs an advantage – the one who needs a difference. This carrot is very immense. The whole seeker community always has these carrots in front of them. In all the books, all the teachers, they give you this carrot. 99.99% of the teachers talk about the knowing and the advantage in it. Nisargadatta said there's only one out of one billion who transcends that.

But for the inner businessman, this is his best deal. He gives so much attention to be in the state of just knowing. That's a Zen satori. Before there was one who sat in front of the wall and later there's only sitting left without the one who sits. So, you have a little satisfaction experience, like an orgasm. Like in sex there is a moment of the absence of the fucker. The whole world is fucking for that little absence. For that you make so much effort! Then you want to have it again and again, you become a junkie. That the fucker goes and only fucking remains. That's tantra.

And if that's your goal, I have nothing against it. But if you ask me if that's reality, I would say, no. Because what-you-are was never fucking at all and never needs to get rid of the fucker. The one who wants to get rid of the fucker is again a hidden fucker.

Q: The seer is the seen...

K: The seer, the seeing and the scene are not different. But in nature there is only scene. But even calling it that creates a difference. It's still part of the dream and only in dream there are levels and advantages and comfort and discomfort. All of that is only in dream. And you have to experience yourself in both, comfort and discomfort, that's what-you-are. When there's discomfort, you are in hell, when there's comfort, you are in heaven. But you cannot have only one. When there is a knower, the separation experience that would be hell.

Q: Ramesh used to say life can only have a rigorous imprisonment or a simple imprisonment...

K: I would say the same. The relative advantage and that already means a disadvantage. You cannot attain what-you-are in whatever way.

Q: Ramesh's teaching made me more open to anything, that's why I am here and listening...

K: Whatever you have done is a preparation for this moment and he was part of it. But I would not give him more credit than your school teacher or anyone else. I would not give anyone credit for anything. All of that was needed so that you can sit here and listen. But there was no special moment. Every moment, every breathing, every sip of coffee, whatever happened before led you to this. You can't miss any one of that.

Whatever happened before made this wood dry enough to light the fire of the heart. You cannot find any special moment that did that. Everything leads to the moment so that the spark lit the fire of what-you-are. And if there is that fire, you burn by nature. And only that fire can burn all ideas. Nothing can resist the fire of Heart. But it is the coolest fire you cannot experience. It's not a fire that burns anything. It's the coolness itself. It's the carelessness of what-you-are. It's not like the fire of karma yoga that burns all concepts. Just by being what-you-are, none of that needs to go. So, it burns all the ideas that something has to be different to be what-you-are.

To be what-you-are nothing needs to be burnt. It burns the idea that something has to be burnt by that coolness that nothing can affect you. Whatever happened never has any consequence for what-you-are – never had never will have any consequence for what is your nature. And that is the worst for the phantom. It can deal with all the fires of hell, all the energy effects. But he cannot deal with the coolness itself. He cannot handle it.

The fact that the phantom or the guest can do whatever he likes and it has no effect on That, this phantom cannot take that. This absolute irrelevance of what you do or don't do is absolutely killing you, that no one wants anything from you. That existence doesn't want anything from you, it's absolutely independent of what you do or don't do. You can do or don't do; it gives a shit about it. This coolness kills you. If you understand or not, no one gives a shit about it.

So, be the coolness itself. That's like the knowledge which has no fire of knowledge. That's called peace. It never burnt anything in that what is heart. All the symbols of Jesus with burning heart are misleading. Because then you think that something has to go, something has to be burnt out or the inner sun has to rise so that the inner 'me' which is like the ice will melt away. All the beautiful words are just carrots for you to give attention to it. And it's more than impossible not to follow them because they promise so much. [Mocking] It's a promised land – only then, only then, only then. Only then – when all the concepts are gone, only then – when you see everything as illusion. How many then's can be there?

That's called the 'then' [Zen] meditation.

Q [Another visitor]: The coolness that you described – is it different?

K: Yes. The coolness is different to difference.

Q: And the coolness is?

K: Coolness doesn't even know coolness. It's the nature of different and indifferent but it doesn't know different or indifferent. So, it's not indifferent which is different from different. That's the nature of different, it doesn't know any different. And the nature of indifference doesn't know any indifference. The nature of knowledge doesn't know any knowledge. You cannot attract that coolness in anyway. Nothing is attractive for that. It cannot be tempted by anything. There is a temptation of Christ but never any temptation of what-you-are. For temptation it needs two again. The temptation of Christ is by whatever you do, it will give you the kingdom of the world, of understanding; promising everything.

That's the temptation of all the gurus and all the masters. And you have to follow them, what else can you do? Even if you turn around to not follow them, you still believe that you are better than them. So, following or not following doesn't make any difference. There is a difference but it doesn't make any difference. So, if you are different or indifferent, it doesn't make any difference for what-you-are.

That is the coolness that your nature which can never be altered or changed by whatever. No way of gaining or losing anything in anything. By all the differences of experiences; with and without the experiencer, knower, the knowledge of what-you-are doesn't have anything to gain or to lose. It never makes you more or less as you are – never; as there is never more or less for what-you-are. You have no quantity, you don't count life. Life never counts life, only the counter counts his good and bad experiences. It needs a counter. That's the businessman, the phantom. And he is in business.

But what-you-are is already the owner of whatever-is and whatever-is-not. You are the Absolute owner, the very self, the Brahman – whatever-is and is-not. So, you have nothing to gain in anything and nothing to lose. So, what is there to gain in gaining and to lose in losing? That's the coolness you are. This rest cannot be given or taken away by anything. This peace is so independent of whatever-is and is-not, because this peace is what-is.

That's why I always say, this moment in its nature is the same peace, same silence as whatever you claim to have in the beyond. This is it, not more or less. Whatever-is is this. So, I Am That which Nisargadatta points to That which is That. And there is no second to That. By being That you are the absolute owner of whatever-is and is-not. So, you have nothing to gain or to lose in anything. You experience yourself in losing and in gaining. But in losing you don't lose and in gaining you don't gain.

So, yes there is an experience of losing and there is an experience of gaining. There's an experience of knowing and an experience of not knowing. But in none of that, you lose your knowledge or you gain knowledge. I can just hammer only on that and I do as if you have to understand something. Do you really think I am interested if you understand something? [Laughter] I mean it. I have absolutely no interest of anyone understanding something. If you ask me, I have to say I absolutely give a shit about it, if you understand something or not. And that's why you come here because I don't want anything from you and I don't want to give you anything. There is no transmission here, no giving, no taking, nothing to gain or to lose in all of that. This is for fun, not for anything else. This is pure entertainment and its cool baby. [Laughter] That is being cool. You cannot be a bigger dude than you already are.

Q [Another visitor]: It's like someone trying to understand but is not able to, so there's an irritation...

K: That's a permanent schizophrenia. You cannot experience yourself otherwise. You are the absolute experience of existence as knowledge and the relative experience of the knower, knowing, what can be known. This realization works like that; there is no other way other than schizophrenia. The whole realization cannot be other than schizophrenic experiences. How can it be otherwise? You experience yourself as that what-you-are. Here-now there's an absolute experience of unpronounced 'I Am' – that you are that knowledge. Then there's a dream of a knower, knowing, what can be known; seer, seeing, what can be seen. Even if that is seen, it's still schizophrenic. So what? That's the way it is.

But you only want to have it one way; you want to stay in that knowledge. You want to drop what is in front of you. No! I have to sit here again like Ramana who tells you – You have to realize yourself, you cannot stop it. And it is going to be quite a long while. So, you better enjoy yourself because it's going to take a while; longer than you can imagine. Can you take that? Even trying to take that is too much; you don't have to take that. Just be what-you-are. You don't have to take that, you don't have to understand that, by being what-you-are. Understanding may happen or not, who fucking cares?

Q [Another visitor]: The sense of feeling lighter, is that also schizophrenic?

K: Of course, it is schizophrenic.

Q [Another visitor]: Are you saying that the Absolute knowledge that you-are is not knowable?

K: It is knowable but not relatively. You cannot say, you don't know yourself. You know yourself by heart – uninterrupted; by being what-you-are. There is no moment, no presence or absence without your being That. That knowledge what-you-are is independent of any presence or absence. That is what-you-are here-now; in whatever so-called presence. So, you are with and without.

You cannot know yourself in any relative way because the knower and what can be known, do not exist. That what is Absolute existence is that what-you-are. It never needs to know to exist but it realizes itself in knower, knowing, what can be known. But you are in the presence of that and in the absence of that.

That there can be a presence of the seer, seeing what can be seen, you have to be That. And you are That, what you cannot not be. So, you are with and without. The Absolute dreamer is with dreaming and without dreaming. And when he starts dreaming, he dreams himself as a dreamer, dreaming, what can be dreamt.

As father, spirit and son. But only Heart is real.

So, you are that what is the Heart, Knowledge, *chit*, ananda – call it whatever – underwear. And this is the way you realize yourself.

Q: What is Heart?

K: You can call it essence, your very nature. Your spiritual heart, not your pumping station. Two centimeters below your solar plexus. That was a joke from Ramana but everyone took it literally. He was just saying that if someone asks you – Who was it? You would say – I was it. [Pointing to heart] When you point to what-you-are, you point to [Pointing at heart] I was it. You do not say I was it by pointing to your head. You point to an imaginary center. You don't point to an idea, you point to that what-you-are.

Q: You call it as essence, the imaginary center...

K: Call it essence, call it That what you are, call it your nature, *Parabrahman*, Shiva – many names. And that knowledge cannot be lost. And since it cannot be lost, it cannot be found again. That's the whole problem with what-you-are, you cannot lose yourself. But now you imagine that you have lost yourself and by your almighty imagination, you take that as real. You are the almighty dreamer and whatever you dream as real becomes Reality and now you dream yourself as a fucking human and you believe in it. And I sit here and tell you – come on!

Any moment you are not what-you-are, giving reality to the dream object, you are missing what-you-are. That's called the misery of the 'me'. The me-ssing of the 'me'. The Shiva becomes a *jiva* and the *jiva* is missing its nature as Shiva. The moment Shiva knows Shiva, he's already a *jiva*. Then the whole story starts. Now I'm sitting here and talking to Shiva and telling him, come on you have never lost yourself in the experience of waking up. No one woke up, nothing happened in the beginning and nothing happens now.

I can only point to that and the best pointer is I don't take any personal bullshit as real, I talk directly to what I Am – 'I' to 'I' and not making it like you have to open your heart or understand something. I give a fuck about if you understand it or not. That's actually talking to myself that never needs to understand to be what-it-is. I absolutely give no attention to any relative bullshit of what has to be done or can be done or will be done or any relative advantage.

I am talking to That what never needs an advantage. That's the absolute advantage, being That what-you-are which never needs or doesn't need anything to be what-it-is. When I say everything else is shit; everything else compared to what-you-are is shit. Being *chit*, you don't know anything. That is *sat-chit-ananda*. It's not three. When you are *Sat*, you are *Sat* not knowing *Sat*. There is no *Sat* for what-you-are. When you are *chit*, you are *chit* not knowing *chit*. There is no knower in *chit*. When you are ananda, there is ananda without any experience of ananda. There is joy without enjoying.

But I can repeat it and repeat it and thank God it doesn't make any difference. [Laughter] And you can understand and understand and you forget it. And maybe in one split-second you see … [Blowing in the wind] Understanding comes and goes, so what? You just stay as you are – cool.

That's what Ramana calls – Abide in that, what never needs to abide in itself. That is paradox – just being that what never needs to be what-it-is. There is no effort; it's an effortlessness of being what-you-are. It never needs anything. It's like abiding in That what never needs to abide and no brain can catch that. You think – He abides in that what never needs to abide in itself. How can I do that? There is no doing in it. It can never be done – never needs to be done.

These are the koans I like from the Zen teachers: unbreakable. It breaks only when you give a shit about whether one is or is-not, knowing or not knowing.

Q [Another visitor]: I had a question but that is shit compared to what you just talked about...

K: That's the joy of shit. I don't tell you forget the shit, I tell you enjoy the shit. Enjoy that it's only shit. Enjoy the emptiness of experiences that it cannot give anything to you. It cannot give or take anything. That's the joy of shit. If there really would be something besides the shit, if there would be one understanding that can give you something, that would be hell.

Q: There is a story that whosoever came to Buddha, he would ask him to be with him for one year before asking a question...

K: They were written three hundred years later.

Q: So, they may not be true?

K: I don't know but I just doubt everything. I even doubt myself – especially myself, from the beginning. And I ask you to do that as well. Doubt even the first notion of 'I', the very self. Doubt that. Be the absolute doubter, even doubting the doubting. Doubt whatever can be doubted and doubt even that. Just stay in the absolute doubt.

Q: What was his intention?

K: I think Buddha had the same intention that I have, not being bothered by someone. [Laughter] Papaji told fifty people that they got it only maybe because he could not see their faces anymore. [Laughter]

Q: He gave the oneness experience to many and they lost it...

K: Papaji said no one got it from me; no one came to me who deserved it. They all should burn in hell. I would say the same. No one who ever came to me got it and whoever claims that he got it from me should burn in hell. I mean it and he meant it.

What has anyone done to deserve something? No one ever deserved anything. What was ever your action? What have you done to sit here? What is not done by the absolute existence? Who claims to have done something and by his effort understood something?

Who got this insight or awakening? Who deserved it? No one. It's all pearls for swines.

He said I am sending ambassadors all over. But now these ambassadors have become kings and they should burn for that. They all claim that Papaji told them to do what they are doing. All have a picture on top of them, like a prostitute who needs a pimp for pushing up. Who needed the confirmation and now claim that I am now in lineage of Ramana? He was one of the rare ones who said that the Self had no lineage and whoever has a lineage is for sure bogus and false. Now they all have lineages of Ramana and Nisargadatta who said that with me all the lineages end. Nisargadatta said What I Am has no lineage and with me all the lineages end. What I Am never had any master and never needed one.

And what comes out of it? [Mocking] In the name of my guru, he asked me to talk. [Laughing] Maybe he asked him to shut up. Ramana always said be quiet and see, not talk and see. [Laughter] I like to make fun about everything.

It's all what-you-are and then you see how stupid you are. There is no limit of stupidity. It's an absolute stupidity and in that you realize yourself. The moment you realize yourself, you can only realize yourself in ignorance. So, whatever you experience is ignorance and I tell you be happy about it. You can only experience yourself in worries. So, be happy and worry. Inquire, but be what-you-are. This paradox is what-you-are. You have to realize yourself inspite of the fact that you are always realized.

But you still have to experience yourself in shit, as *chit*. And I tell you be happy that you can only experience yourself as shit. Be happy you can never experience yourself as Knowledge because if you could experience yourself as knowledge, there would be two and knowledge could be owned. Then you really would be fucked. Be happy that it is impossible to know yourself in any relative way. And whoever claims that he knows himself – fuck up his... [Laughter]

Some people ask why do you put every teacher down? What is more fun? Holding them up is much too heavy. Putting them down, they fall by themselves. [Laughter] It's more an action of laziness not of necessity. Laziness is your nature. Be what-you-cannot-not-be and that is laziness of the laziest. Be That what is the *jñani* but don't know any *jñani*. And the one who knows himself as a *jñani* are sure two *jñanis* too many.

In India, they say that the place where the flame comes from is always very cool. The fire and the experience of fire comes from that origin but the origin stays absolutely cool. It never experiences or gets affected by anything. Now the experience that you get burned is an imaginary experience. In that experience no one gets burned, never did. It's like a Bunsen burner, the flame always has fire but the burner is always cool. So, be the Absolute Bunsen burner. [Laughter] But you don't have to try to be cool. You are cool anyway.

Q [Another visitor]: It is so simple here-now and yet it is so difficult that one in a million gets it. Why is that?

K: You can say it's easy to just be what-you-are in this fearlessness. But the moment you step out, it jumps in again; the openness and the tunnel-view.

Q: What is that which gets in?

K: It's like a ping-pong. Here you can just be what-you-are inspite of the ping-pong, you don't care. But when you get out, you are by your own. The fear steps in and you cannot not take it seriously. Then you are again in the story of the 'me'.

Q: And then there is a time that it switches forever?

K: No.

Q: It can never be forever?

K: No because there's still time involved. So, you have to be here and there what-you-are and you are That. So, it doesn't have to change. No one ever got it. I wouldn't even say that one in one billion gets it.

Q: Maharaj used to say one in a million gets it...

K: I would say no one got it. Not even one in a hundred billion. No one was ever not it, so no one ever got it. As no one lost it, no one can get it back. So, no one ever got it, not even one. I would rather say, not even one got it. Everyone is it but no one can get it. That's all.

Q: No one gets it is different than no one owns it...

K: It's the same ownership idea. Someone got it means someone earned it.

Q: So, you cannot get it but you can only be it?

K: You cannot not be it. But you cannot have it. Being it is fine, having it is hell.

Q [Another visitor]: This moment will come back again and again?

K: It cannot come back, it will never be gone.

Q: And the Self experiences itself again and again?

K: That's the dream that a moment comes and goes. But in coming nothing comes and in going nothing goes. The next moment is already there, it cannot come and the last moment is still there, it cannot go. There's a dream of coming and going. But in coming nothing comes and in going nothing goes. You can say that this absolute moment is the absolute potential of all the future and past. This moment contains everything whatever can be the future or the past and it's still there.

You think it's like a painting that is always there. No. Everything is already there in the potential. In that absolute dreamer, the absolute potential, the whole realization is complete. So, even when he is not realizing, not dreaming, the whole dream is still there. The dreamer, the dreaming whatever can be dreamt; whatever can be is there in the absolute potential of *Parabrahman*.

But now you think that this is like an infinite painting and you have to look at this painting again and again. You want to fix it in the moment but you cannot. I can just point to the absolute nature of life, which is the absolute potential in its absence and presenting itself to itself in absolute presence of nothing coming and nothing going. Because that what is the presenter, the presenting and what can be presented is already there in its absolute potential before even presenting itself.

So, in waking up nothing wakes up, in sleeping nothing sleeps, in going nothing goes, in coming nothing comes. That's the silence which is the nature of the nature. No coming, no going.

Q: But this moment is coming again and again...

K: It's never coming and never going because it's already there in the potential. So, it doesn't come when you experience it. It's already there before you even experience it.

Q: Is it the potential or the realization?

K: It is in potential and in realization infinite. What's the difference?

Q: No difference...

K: So, it never comes in coming and doesn't go in going. So, there's only silence and silence is what-you-are. It's not a silence that is prior to something or in a different realm. This is the silence right now. You are the silence who experiences silence. You are the absolute experiencer experiencing what-you-are, as silence. As there's only silence and that's the nature of what-you-are. Self can only experience itself and Self is infinite in nature. So, whatever you experience is Self and it is infinite in its nature. There's nothing but Self and you don't have to understand that.

Q: I don't get that this moment comes again and again...

K: You say I don't get it because you want to have it. You want to own it, the greedy 'me'. That makes you stupid. Greediness makes you stupid. Trying to have it, trying to own it; that's stupidity. You want to own something what can never be owned. You want to put it in your bloody brain and take it home, what can never be taken by anyone. You cannot own it. You want to have this understanding forever. The realization of this moment cannot be taken to the next moment. It's only for this moment. You cannot have it after ten days. It has to stay in this moment. It's not as if you can get any understanding in future moments from this moment. But you want to put it in your pocket just-in-case you may need it later. Just-in-case, as an insurance. You even buy books for that. You think if you don't understand it, then you can buy books in case I need it.

You are booked out. You want to book your future. You want to have a journey with no unexpected moments. You already want to know how you would die. Everyone runs to astrologers and wants to know what would happen in ten years and when will I die and how much money will I make and who will like me and what should I do about it. All because of what? Because you want to control something because you think you need to control. Even to try to control life is a joke and you know it by heart that it's a joke to control. But you try.

This joke you cannot stop. You always try to control life. You want to charm God; you want to charm existence because you think if I know more, if I understand it better, I can control existence. I can charm it, I can manipulate it. You become a little manipulator, a money-pull-later. I put something in the ATM and I pull it later. My knowledge bank, my understanding bank. And I want to get it back with interest. My consciousness should grow in that, it should not be less. It's amazing – this little banker inside. Then you go to Ramesh Balsekar, the divine banker. [Laughter]

What a joke. The absolute owner that owns everything starts to count little cents and pennies and is afraid that someone cheats him. If the rickshaw driver takes one rupee more, then he starts shouting. That's the tradition of all the seekers. Stingy bloody seekers, kick them all, give them nothing and leave them nowhere. [Laughter] That's what I would do if I was a rickshaw driver in India.

Q [Another visitor]: What is the difference between absence and silence?

K: Absence needs an absence of presence to be absence. Silence doesn't need any presence of absence or absence of absence to be silence. That's the nature of silence. It's independent of any presence absence absence presence absence absence presence absence.

Q: People think absence is silence...

K: It's a nice trap. It's an experience of silence but the experience of silence is not silence. It's a relative experience of silence but not silence. That relative experience of silence is dependent on absence of a presence. It's like time and no-time.

February 11, 2013
Mumbai, India

Chapter Eight

There Is No Attainment, Only Entertainment

~

Q: I would love to ask a question that wouldn't come from the phantom but it seems there is none...

K: We are all used to second-hand questions. There are only second-hand questions, hear-say. There is no other way; it has to be hear-say. No one will ever create a new question. Impossible! All questions are already asked and all the answers are already given.

Q: It has already happened, how can we show our appreciation of your presence here except only by asking more stupid questions?

K: That's for fun. That's how you realize yourself, without expectation. You have questions and they don't have to be good.

Q: They just pop-up?

K: They are just there when they are there and they get answered or not. But when you come with an expectation and you try to ask a question which gives you something, then it's hard work and then you get punished for that. Questions and answers are just free flow of energy. There's no need for any result. One triggers the other: The question is a reaction of all what happened before and the answer is just a reaction on that reaction. That's all. There is no necessity or any need that something comes out of it.

But if you expect something to come out, that by the answer you understand something and by that understanding you can get somewhere, and maybe by that understanding you even know yourself, then you are in trouble. Otherwise it's just entertainment. Question-answer entertainment. Sometimes the answer pleases you and sometimes not. But at the end I can point infinitely on that – that what-you-are never needs to be pleased and never needs to get something out of it.

And it seems like after a while, you cannot get enough of – that you cannot get anything and you don't need anything. That's what is called good company because there is no business running. There is nothing to get and nothing to give. No gaining, no losing. Everything is – you don't even know what. That's the nature of meditation, that's the way Reality realizes itself. That's your natural state. Your natural state is meditation: experiencing yourself infinitely.

The artificial one is the 'being' who expects something from whatever happens. That makes you an artificial self. The Self cannot stop realizing itself moment-by-moment. But there was never any Self which gained anything in that way. So, there was never any gaining and never any losing in it. Moment-by-moment the next sip of coffee, the next question, the next answer... never ending story of That reacting to itself.

I don't transmit anything here; I have no intention to teach something, I don't give you anything. That's why you are attracted to this company. Because that is an attraction beyond your imagination. What-you-are is attracted to the peace that there is nothing to gain. No one wants anything from me; you may call it as that acceptance which you are longing for. That's acceptance in action or Self in action.

Q [Another visitor]: Sometimes we might feel uneasy around you, is that also because the phantom wants something from you?

K: Of course. You expect something and then you don't get it. Then you feel not at ease. That's only your problem. I see it, but I wouldn't change any inch of what 'I Am' or how 'I Am'. The coolness is too much for you. The coolness that nobody cares about how you are, that's not so easy for this little 'me'.

I can only be like I Am – careless. I have no intention of pleasing anyone, not even this guy [Pointing to himself]. If he's pleased – okay, if not – that's okay too. If you are pleased that's okay, if not, please-off. [Laughing] And I really over react sometimes on people who really want to control me or want to give me a structure or try to make me feel guilty. Then I really get overboard, it really gets worse. Then the little Karl comes up, the one that's pissed.

Q [Another visitor]: Pure nakedness – without attributes...

K: Even nakedness is an attribute, it's one too many. Nakedness is still one concept too many. Just pronouncing it is too much. Naked as you are. But what would that be? That what has no clothes, no form. But even no form is no form too many. Whatever you try is futile.

Q [Another visitor]: But at the same time you spend so much energy answering questions...

K: I don't spend energy. Do you feel that I use energy when I give an answer?

Q: You have a really gruesome schedule...

K: But if I spend energy, I would be exhausted like hell. I am more energetic after the talk than before. It's true. I can be tired before but I am not tired after-words. When I have to be quiet that makes me tired. Just spitting it out when it comes, without hesitation, without care doesn't exhaust you. You can only get exhausted when you want to make it a teaching or make it really true or right or that it has to be sound enough that people cannot attack it anymore. Then you are in trouble. Then I would be exhausted even before

I sit here. Because then I would fear that maybe today I am not in the right energy or something. [Laughter]

That's an idea many people have – today I am not energetic enough to do that, maybe today the beasts are too strong for me. And you are always surrounded by beasts, you know that. The moment you give a little bit of weakness, they bite you – immediately. They don't come for someone who is weak; they come for someone whom they can attack. No it's fun.

Q [Another visitor]: What does weakness look like?

K: If I would go to your level that would be weakness. You wanted to know it, now you got it. [Laughter] Everyone wants to put you down to his suffering business, to his little understanding business, to his little basis, his little home. Where he knows what to do, he knows where the furniture is. And if I would go to his level; he would know how to kill me. Everyone is like a little killer, I tell you. Especially women they want to put you down to their level. Not for nothing I don't like them. [Laughter]

Q [A woman]: But we can't believe it…

K: Because I am a rare man that says it, everyone else thinks it.

Q [Another visitor]: Yesterday I felt that there is truth that people are lashing back and attacking you…

K: Of course. The worse scenario is in Tiruvannamalai, all these so-called chai-shop masters. For ten years I was sitting there. Normally I like this fighting, but after a while I just got bored. It's boring fighting for who is right and how Ramana was. Everyone trying to make a religion out of Ramana, I tried to destroy it. But they still kept coming back. I really got tired fighting against Ramana-ism. Making a new Jesus out of Ramana is just another joke. What to do?

That I like about Nisargadatta. There is no one who could make a Jesus out of Nisargadatta. He was nasty enough and naughty enough. Sorry Ramana, you were too polite. [Laughter] Only in the kitchen he was angry but people rarely saw him in the kitchen.

So, anyone wants to attack me? I am ready.

Q[Another visitor]: I have a question about personal perception. I feel emotions of people around me and I feel over-loaded...

K: When you have healthy personality, your armor is so thick that the emotions cannot go through. That would be like a totally established person in the field of personality. Then your filter system is total and the emotions cannot penetrate. You are like a knight with a big armor around you – defense system. A very healthy personality is when the defense system is really strong, no one can touch him. He can be like a bull-dozer.

But when the perception is shifting and not completely established, you become very fragile. When you go to the personal perception, all the emotions go to you. The moment you take it personal, then they get you. It actually kills you. This means your back door is open. It comes from the front and it has to go through. It should be like – welcome, well-go and not like welcome, oh shit! [Laughter]

Q: But in my case it happens this way...

K: Then you take it personal and then it becomes too much. Taking it personal and making a story out of it. Having a personal point of perception is nothing bad. When you have an open front door and open back door, then it's no problem. You cannot get tired by that. But if you have an open front door but your back door is closed...

Q: Back door opens sometimes later...

K: Yeah, in the meanwhile you collect.

Q: When it's too much the back door opens...

K: That's the laziness you-are. When you are the laziness, it's like a wind passing through... puff... puff... That's why I liked it when they called me Swami pouf-pouf. It's like a fresh breeze. If you don't make a concept of good energy or bad energy, then it's just like a breeze. Sometimes when I see a reaction, I give it back. I am just generous of giving it back and not keeping it to myself of what they want to get rid of.

Normally everyone wants to get rid of something, some aggression, emotions and they look for someone who wants it. It's like when two girls meet they ask – How are you today? They are just checking if she is ready to give or ready to take today. [Laughter] When there are two givers, there is no conversation but when there is one giver and one taker, then there's a conversation. One gives a lot and other one takes it. [Laughter] Then the one who takes it gets home loaded and the one who gives goes shopping. One goes dropping and other goes shopping.

Last week I spoke about the magic business everywhere. Giving and taking and all of that. Even when people try to take something, they try to control the giver because they want to be the best 'takers'. The giver can only come to them – I am the best listener. What to do?

Actually it's not in your hand if the back door is open or not.

Q: Sometimes I see someone taking things so personally that I laugh and they feel offended. I am not laughing at the person but it's a natural reaction...

K: I laugh at the person and the one that's behind it. And you do the same, you laugh at the person. Don't say you don't laugh at him. You are not better than me, no! [Laughter] Then they say, I come to you with my serious problem and you are laughing. I will never come to you again. And I think that's what I want. Go and dump your rubbish somewhere else. It's all rubbish. It's all emotional rubbish from yesterday and they want to get rid of it. Then you become like a rubbish dump. Then they deserve that you laugh at them because that's the only way of dealing with them. The sense of humor, that's the only way of letting it pass like the wind.

This is like an exercise of a sense of humor, that you start laughing at everything – outside, inside, everywhere. [Laughter] That you especially laugh at the joker who wakes up in the morning, who takes it personal or not. Then he claims that he knows something or not. That joker you should laugh at instantly when he wakes up. It's like – he again – he, he, he.

Q [Another visitor]: Is that the armor?

K: The armor is something else. It's your fear defense system – your stiffness. Then sometimes existence wants to have a joke with you and you fall in love with someone. Then you open up again. Then sooner or later it shows you that you should have rather been closed. But existence knows the tricks to open you – just for one person maybe. Maybe for your baby and then sometimes the baby gets crucified.

Q [Another visitor]: It seems to be a good thing to not have the armor...

K: I wouldn't say it is good. If that would be good, the other would be not good. I have no idea what's good or bad in it. If it's like that, it is like that. If not, it's the opposite. For me it makes no difference for what-you-are, it only makes difference for ideas, for the concept of 'me' which is open. [Mocking] An open heart is better than a closed heart. Ha... ha... ha...!

When you have an open heart, everyone puts his rubbish into it, you know that. [Laughter]

Armor or no-armor is all part of the dream story. If really what-you-are wants the armor to be broken or the heart knot to go, if the phantom really has to be broken, then you can wait forever. That's an infinite story of the ownership of consciousness – of this love affair. There will always be different ways of controlling. Even by trying not to control, you control. It's an infinite, trying to know yourself or controlling yourself – out of love. And there's no way out!

Then you think an open heart is better than a closed heart because then I am already open to myself. 'I' am open to 'myself'. Just let this sentence go to your ears – 'I am open to myself'. [Mocking] Fuck me now, I am open, I am ready. You are not coming? Bloody self! No one was so open as me. No one's heart was as open as my heart. There's a competition of 'open hearts' everywhere, especially in Byron bay. [Laughter] It's an open heart bay.

No. What we can talk about is the dream. The dream character has a story. What to do with it? And it's already written. There's no way and no need to change it. So, you have to be with and without that guest. That guest which wakes up in the morning will always have a different story. And one is as silly as the other one.

Q [Another visitor]: You said what-you-cannot-not-be is not awareness because that comes late...

K: I didn't say that. I said awareness is not a special thing for what-you-are. You are not more in awareness than this so-called unconscious state. But still you are what-you-are in awareness. But you will not know yourself in awareness or in any other state. There is no advantage of awareness or disadvantage.

Q: Is it a perception or are they just words?

K: What-you-are is not even a perception. You are That what is perception but you are not perception. Some have the concept that awareness is perception and then in that screen of perception projections are happening, perceiver perceiving what can be perceived. They take that as the real nature. They call the screen which is perception as always pure and in that all the illusory sensations happen – like a dance of information. It sounds good. But I'm sorry, it's still a dream.

To know yourself as that perception, the screen, the awareness, is still too much. Because the moment you know yourself as that, you divide yourself from something else. When I say it's too late, the definer is already there. The definer that defined himself. Even the purest awareness, the purest notion of 'I' needs a definer. That's the finest you can define yourself as. But it's not fine enough for what-you-are.

Aurobingo would call it the supreme consciousness. But even the supreme consciousness is not supreme enough. The highest is not high enough for what-you-are. Because you are That what is the highest which doesn't know any highest or lowest. You are That which is your nature, which never knows any differences in anyway. There is no higher or lower in what-you-are. But if you take that as the highest, you instantly make all other things as lower.

So, you can say that you experience yourself as the highest, but it doesn't make you the highest. You experience yourself as the lowest, but it doesn't make you the lowest. You experience yourself as whatever, a dream character or whatever can be experienced. But experiencing yourself as a phantom Karl doesn't make you the phantom. Experiencing yourself as born, doesn't make you born. No experience makes you that what you experience. And awareness is already an experience – the beginning of realization. But the beginning of the realization is not the Reality – not different, but it's not that what-you-are in nature.

What else can I point to? It's so simple and it's not needed to be understood. You can never lose that. But you still sit here thinking that by understanding, you can gain it. It's amazing! But why not? It's like 'why' again and 'why not' again. It's like a sport – ping-pong. An infinite ping-pong – ping the question and pong the answer. Sometimes it's pong-ping or ping-ping.

Q [Another visitor]: It's all in the illusion, so it's not relevant...

K: Only an illusion would call something else as an illusion. Many people think that I see everything as a dream, the whole world, the whole universe, all is illusion. Then you can ask them, but who is saying this? One illusion saying everything is illusion and another illusion that sees everything as not an illusion. Just two different polarities and they will talk forever about who is right. If I would say everything is an illusion, for sure someone else can say, how can you say that? And both would be wrong.

That's what I like. Everything what could be said is wrong. Even what is not said is wrong.

Q [Another visitor]: Nothing should be said...

K: Then he thinks he's right. [Laughter]

Q: But that's what you meant...

K: No. That was not what I meant. That's exactly what I'm pointing at – the conclusion business. I conclude that if saying is bad then not saying is good. That's 'me' – the conclusion, finding out that if I'm quiet, I'm safe. Doesn't work. It may work for few moments, but then you are back in business.

You say one thing and I just say the opposite, just to show you the ridiculous stand point. Both are as stupid as they can be. Even awareness, even the highest spiritual concept, any golden cow you can come up with, any conclusion of scientific truth – is all ignorance. Thank God! All is ignorance. Even you are ignorance.

But you can say that – that there can be ignorance, you have to be. And That you can call knowledge. But That what is knowledge doesn't have any idea of knowledge. You are in ignorance as what-you-are in knowledge because even the knowledge that you can imagine, is ignorance. Thank God!

And I say you should be absolutely happy that you cannot know yourself. Whatever you can know – especially the knower, knowing, what can be known – is what? Empty for what-you-are. It doesn't make you more or less as what-you-are. It's all empty shit. Thank God! You are the quality itself. You are the gold that doesn't need any gold, to know. And that what needs some gold in his pocket is a beggar compared to what-you-are.

Any little knowledge that you claim to have or anything, your little home where you entered or landed, is bullshit! You are the palace itself. But every home is like a beggar's home. Any famous home, every golden cow, is a shitty cow. Cow shit – that you can own, but not That what is existence. Isn't it fantastic?!

But you become a beggar the moment you believe that you earned something, you know something, you have some knowledge. At that very moment, you become a beggar begging for – whatever. And then you defend your little bowl of skull where you put all your bullshit insights. [Laughter] That's why in black tantra they have the skull, like the black sun. But even the black sun is not that what is the sun.

Then people are begging for answers. If I would deliver them the answers, I would be the same beggar, trying to sell bullshit.

Q [Another visitor]: Is this thing called body really nothing?

K: It's still a piece of meat. It's now a piece of meat and later it's still a piece of meat – food body.

Q: People think that body has the answers...

K: Yeah. The body is the answer. The body doesn't have an answer because the body doesn't own anything, but the body is the answer. You can take your little finger as your master. If you ask it – How are you today? [Pause] You can wait the whole day and there will be silence. The body knows much more than you. Your little finger never had any question. So, it is actually your guru. You are surrounded by your guru. Total wisdom in your little finger.

Q: So, who has the questions?

K: Suzy!

Q: But Suzy is the body...

K: No!

Q: So, what is Suzy?

K: Suzy is even when there is out of body experience. How many times people have this out of body experience. So, they cannot be the body. So, what is it that is not this body? It does not depend on the body. Then you can go further, is it the perception – spirit? No, you are even without the spirit. Then you can go to awareness and even there you cannot find Shalaba.

Q: Can you...

K: No. I am not a teacher. Imagine I would sit here so that you would learn something and I would give an answer to your question. Now we get into that trap again. You want to reason about where is Suzy. Is it the body that is the problem? Now we start again from scratch as if nothing ever happened, back to kindergarten. After so many years with UG, Osho, we start from scratch as if nothing ever happened. Stupid as before! I like that. For me, that's magic. You have never learnt anything in your whole life. If totality wanted you to understand something, it would happen inspite of your ability of understanding. And if not, you can try it for infinity and it will not happen. So, what's there to do?

I cannot even say, you are stupid. I just see whatever is the Absolute, doesn't allow you to understand. If the Absolute wants you to understand, you would understand inspite of you even trying. It's amazing! In that sense I don't call you stupid. You are just lived by life as you are lived by life. Life is living you as you are lived by life and you have no way of changing that. But it doesn't make you more or less as you are.

So, in that sense, I am talking to what-I-Am which in that sense the inability to understand something is not different from the ability to understand because both are given. Both are by total demand of what-is and not by one who is stupid enough or is not trying enough. There cannot even be one thought without the total demand of totality. The whole universe is living you. Every thought is given by that totality. Every effect in you is the effect of totality. The whole potential is living itself through you.

Q [Another visitor]: Sometimes you have no energy and suddenly you are filled with energy...

K: You wake up only because totality allows it to happen, otherwise you would sleep forever. It would just give you no energy to wake up anymore; you would remain a corpse forever. Sudden child deaths are very common, total recall for the baby. No one knows why the baby died, it just stopped breathing. It's very common. The whole scientific world don't know what happened. Why that baby and not the other one? I like that. It's just like – okay, bye, bye, recall.

Q: The other day you said many cars are not made well...

K: Some cars are not even made for a week. They have to go back even before they are made.

Q: And what about the cars here?

K: They are out of fashion! [Laughter]

Everyone comes for that. Without that Absolute acceptance which is the Self, you cannot even lift your little finger. I cannot say one word without the total acceptance of life. Whatever I say may sound different but I could be not different if it would not be allowed by That. Ramesh would call it God's will. For me, it's like a block of existence, it is as it is. It cannot be different as it already is. There is no will involved. No one had any 'will' or created anything. It is just as it is. Every moment is already there and you have to experience yourself moment-by-moment. Never ending story. And not one moment is better than the other one, in nature.

The next sip of coffee is as good as the next enlightenment. Einstein's relativity theory is not better than a sip of coffee. And the whole scientific world is still jerking around with it – trying to prove it. And it's nothing, just another idea of ignorance. Later Einstein was fighting with quantum theory – God doesn't play dice... Ha... ha... ha...

The Knowledge has nothing to gain or to lose if you are intelligent or not. If you are intelligent, it's okay, if not, that's okay too. The Knowledge doesn't become more intelligent when it makes you intelligent or how it lives you. There is nothing to gain in the way you are. If you understand something or you have a deep insight of your imaginary nature in meditation, it gives a shit about it.

That's what-you-are – nothing to gain and nothing to lose in any – underwear. [Laughter] That's called peace. To be that which has nothing to gain or to lose in anything. Nothing makes you more, nothing makes you less. Being more stupid or the absolute stupid guy on earth doesn't make you less as you are; or more, if you believe to be the highest enlightened ass-hole. That I like. All the realized ones that awakened and know their true nature, they are as much fucking ass-holes as everyone. Then you can say that they can only be as they are by the demand of totality.

I read a message on a rickshaw a few years ago – "No one remains a virgin, sooner or later life fucks everyone". Even the most pure and virgin spirit, sooner or later has a dirty idea. That's how life fucks you. It will show you how pure and virgin you are.

It's the last talk, it's now or never. But even that would be a concept. I would say if you cannot be what-you-are today, you will never become it in any future. So, it's now or never. But you are now and never.

Q [Another visitor]: Why did you make a distinction between 'now or never' and 'now and never'...

K: It's neither now or never. That what-you-are is not now and it's not never. It's not even never. It if would be now, it would be fixed on the 'now'. If it would be never, it would be fixed on 'never'. It's neither now or never. There is only a 'now' because you-are and there is only a 'never' because you-are. There is only eternity because you-are and there is only this moment because you-are. But you are not in the eternity and you are not in the now.

For what-you-are there is neither now or eternity. So, you are neither in the now or in the eternity. All you can come up with are – polarities, comparisons. *Neti-neti*, neither-neither. So, stay where you cannot-not-be – That you can never find, that you can never know what it is. Self-Abidance – take a bite in yourself.

Q: What is self-abidance?

K: Being what-you-cannot-not-be. That is self-abidance. Being that what never needs to abide in itself. Because that what-you-are never needs to stay anywhere or establish itself in anything to be what-it-is. We are talking about the power of discrimination. That what discriminates is not what-you-are and that which does not discriminate is not what-you-are. You are neither the discriminator neither the non-discriminator. There is discrimination in discriminating and non-discriminating. So, even the non-discriminating is not what-you-are. This paradox you cannot grasp, in any way.

Q [Another visitor]: Can we do that with impersonal and personal awareness?

K: You can do that with everything. Whatever you say, there has to be an opposite.

Q [Another visitor]: And self-abidance is non-abidance?

K: Being the absolute not knowing the absolute, being what-you-cannot-not-be. And there is no possibility of not being that.

Q: Self-abidance is just a word...

K: It is a pointer to That what never needs to abide in itself. It has to be a paradox. For me there is no self-abidance. But if you ask me what it means, it means be that what-you-cannot-not-be which never needs to abide in anything. Because the self never needs to abide in itself because the self never even knows the self. And without knowing any self or no-self there is no need to abide in anything. And by being that what never needs or doesn't need anything, you are what you cannot-not-be. So, it's not a relative 'me' abiding in a special state. That Ramana calls it a natural state. It is so natural that it's your very nature which doesn't need to know the nature – what-it-is and what-it-is-not. That's your natural state of knowledge. Being the knowledge which doesn't know knowledge never needs to know itself. And the knower who tries to know himself or whatever can be known will always be a phantom and there's no bridge between that.

There no scientific or Vedanta or anyway to attain what-you-are – never-ever. There is only entertainment, not at-tainment.

Q [Another visitor]: So what-you-are cannot do anything about it, what you say, what you know. You cannot do anything but simply keep silence?

K: No. It doesn't need to keep silence, that's the beauty of it. Silence doesn't need silence to keep silence. And that what needs silence is another phantom alone – a phantom silence. Peace doesn't need peace. So, peace-off. Knowledge doesn't need anything to know – no knower, no knowing, nothing needs to be known. So, knowledge-off – forget knowledge and be what-you-are. Truth never needs truth, so truth-off.

Q: What you are, you cannot talk about...

K: I can talk about it day and night, it makes no difference. I Am what I Am talking about it or not talking about it. If I should be quiet to be what-I-Am, it would be a shit peace.

Q: I mean, you cannot describe that...

K: I can but only negatively. I can say you can be that what-you-cannot-not-be. That's describing it. But it doesn't help you. It's not a relative description. I can say you cannot not know yourself. You have to be what-you-are, you cannot escape it, you cannot get out of it.

Q: You cannot experience it?

K: You can only experience it absolutely. Without the absolute experience that you are, there would be no relative experiencer. But you will never experience yourself relatively and the Absolute experience that you-are is uninterrupted. The Absolute knowledge that you-are, that even to deny 'to be', you have to be.

Q: You can have only absolute knowledge and absolute experience?

K: No. You can only 'be' absolute knowledge but there is no knower who knows that. If the knower knows or doesn't know, you are inspite of that.

Q: Knowledge without the knower?

K: The knowledge doesn't even need the absence of the knower. Now you make it relative again. Knowledge with or without knower, in whatever, is That what is knowledge. Nothing has to go for it and nothing has to come for it. It is That what-is. But you cannot say knowledge without a knower because then you make it depending on the absence of a knower. Whatever you say, you make it relative. It is neither relative nor not relative. It can be relative when it's relative but it's not relative when it's relative. Nor is it not-relative when it's not relative.

It can experience itself in whatever – relative or not relative, in knowing and the knower. But it never becomes what is experienced. It is already what is experienced; it doesn't have to become it. It is the realizer, it is the realizing, it is what is realized – as That what is Heart. The knowledge realizing itself as the knower, knowing, what can be known. The nature of the knower is not different from the nature of the knowing or what can be known. All of that is what-you-are.

Q: What is the relation between the absolute experience and the relative experience?

K: There is no relation, that's the problem. All is absolute experience. Even the experience of the knower is the absolute experience of the knower. The absolute experience of knowing is the absolute experience of knowing. And the absolute experience of what can be known is the absolute experience. There is only the Absolute experiencing itself. There was never any less than absolute experience and the next sip of coffee is the same absolute experience as whatever.

Q: So, it is the absolute experiencing itself?

K: It cannot experience itself but it is experiencing itself as an experiencer, experiencing what can be experienced. But it can never experience itself. But all of that are absolute experiences. But the experience of the experiencer is not what is the Self. The Self is That what is experiencing itself as an experiencer, but the experiencer is not the Self. It sounds semantics but it is not.

Q: I used to believe in the statement – What can be stated should be stated clearly and what cannot be stated, one should remain quiet about that…

K: That's Wittgenstein. He had a stone up there – Wittgen-stone. [Laughter] He said what you cannot talk about, you should be quiet.

Q: We are doing the later part most of the time…

K: I tell you I never said one word. If you ask what I Am, I never said one word. I never experience myself. What-I-Am is silence itself, how can I say something? But still I realize myself as a talker, talking, what can be talked about. But as what I Am, I never said one word. I am always quiet, totally quiet.

Q [Another visitor]: Maharaj said when I look within, I see that I am nothing and when I look without, I see that I am everything…

K: He said on one side there is love which tells me I am everything, on the other side wisdom tells me I am nothing. And in between, my life flows. It's not outside or inside. Love tells me I am everything is the oneness experience. Wisdom tells me I am nothing. Both cannot be right, both promise something that they cannot deliver. So, I can neither know myself by love or wisdom. That is peace. Normally, you believe one or the other. You try to unify yourself, embrace something, being one with something. The other would be the suicide tendency, becoming nothing, not even to exist. Wisdom tells you that you want to kill yourself. The life tendency and the death tendency – yes and no. The total 'no' to existence and the total 'yes' to existence. But in between, you are. You are neither 'no' or 'yes'. But in that you live yourself. You live yourself in love and in wisdom. Life wish, embracing everything, being alive, being in harmony with yourself. And the death wish, because wisdom tells you when I am not, I cannot be hurt.

So, you try to be in harmony with love or try to be untouched in wisdom. These are the two tendencies and in between that you are. None of the tendencies can make you more or less as you are. But they both tempt you, all the time. Just being quiet and being what-you-cannot-not-be, by looking and seeing, you cannot not give attention to that. They will be there and you have to give attention. So, you give attention but without expecting something out of it. You are inspite-of – neither that nor that.

Q [Another visitor]: Are you saying one should reject both the things?

K: I didn't say reject them. I said see both of them as empty, they cannot make you more or less as you are. Don't reject them. Rejecting is already giving them too much. They are neither good or bad; they are just two ways of realizing yourself – in the tendency of creation and in the tendency of destruction. Shiva in its creation and destruction.

Q: And you follow none of that?

K: No. You have to follow it. But none of them can make you more or less as you are. There is no way of rejecting yourself. You will always have to follow total demand of yourself. You cannot stop yourself because for stopping it needs two and for rejecting it again needs two. You are the love and you are the oneness and you are the wisdom of rejection. You are the nothing and you are the everything. You are not different in nothing and not different in everything. You are That what is nothing and everything. Nothing would be the wisdom and everything would be the love but you are neither love nor wisdom. But still you realize yourself in both.

Q: You can have only three choices. Either you accept both, or you reject both or be indifferent to both…

K: Do whatever you like. Choice is already too late.

Q: No choice?

K: No chooser. Where is the chooser? There are many choices but you cannot find this 'chooser' – this asshole who claims to have a choice. If there would be a chooser, there would be one who can choose before he chooses. If one would have a free will, there would be one who wants what he wants before he wants what he wants. What an idea!

Everyone wants to have a wand, like Harry Potter. Everyone wants to have the biggest wand – I want, I want, I want, I wish, I wish, I wish. It's all wishy-washy.

Q [Another visitor]: So, are you saying there is no chooser?

K: But again, who would see that? Who cannot find the chooser? Who is the 'not finder'? You can do that with everything. Who was the finder before and who is the 'not finder' now? Who was the doer and who is now the non-doer? You always shift between that.

But the pointers are not meant that you shift from doer to a non-doer, chooser to non-chooser, from finder to non-finder. But that's the tendency for everyone. If I can understand and by that understanding, I cannot keep myself as a doer, then I will be a non-doer. I survive as good as a non-doer as a doer – another survivor. And then you think you are better as a non-doer than as a doer. Or, I am a non-seeker, I gave up seeking. I called off the church forever; I don't go to church anymore. I would rather call it – I called off the church and not the search. [Laughter]

Q: So, you can't be the doer or the non-doer or the chooser or non-chooser...

K: You are neither-neither. What is left is what-you-are. You are the absolute leftover, you know that. [Mocking] You cannot eat yourself but you will always be a leftover from yesterday and all the times before. Everything went, but you could not go with it, you still will be what-you-are. The party is over but you are still there and wondering, all these parts, these particles are gone. All the energetic dance of the particles, information of the universe.

And what I like most is that you are the almighty itself and you cannot even make one little decision. [Laughing] You are the absolute knowledge and the moment you know something, you are stupid like hell.

Q [Another visitor]: Hopeless and helpless...

K: That's personal again. You are less than hopeless – hopelessness, wishlessness. Hopeless is still too much hope.

Q [Another visitor]: You say that the whole block has happened outside time...

K: Not outside of time. The whole block is silence.

Q: Is it timeless?

K: It's silence, not even timeless. Silence means nothing ever happened, nothing is ever born, nothing is created and nothing can go. Nothing has ever come and nothing will ever go – that's the pointer of the block. There is no coming in coming and no going in going. There is an experience of coming but by that experience of coming nothing comes. There is an experience of going but by that experience of going nothing goes. That's why it's called the infinite now.

Infinite now means the total loop of existence. The total block of all possible and impossible ways of experiencing yourself. And the dream is that you take coming and going as time and real. That's the dream. It's not that what you experience is not real. That you think that in coming something comes and in going something goes, that is your dream. By that you create time because time means coming and going: something is created and something dies. That is your dream. Then you become that born and dying... whatever.

But in Reality there is a silent block of life. This eternal life which is never born and never dies. This is what-is. That is called Absolute existence, Absolute life, Absolute Self, absolute whatever and there is nothing but That. The pointer of Eternal life is that life is never born and life can never die; and whatever is, is life. There is nothing but life. And you are That – that's all. That's peace. You don't have to call it peace, just be that. There's a satisfaction beyond imagination. That silence is what-you-are and by being That, you are satisfaction itself. Because there is no one left who needs to be satisfied. That's the nature of satisfaction.

So, there's no need and no one left who is or could be satisfied. And if there never was anyone who was satisfied, there was never anyone who was not satisfied. If there's never any possibility of enlightenment, there is never any possibility of un-enlightenment. The dream is dream of enlightenment. By the possibility of knowing, you create the possibility of not knowing. They come together and then you are in the dream of future, of the possibility that one day you can know yourself. Or that you know yourself more than what you already know about yourself.

That Absolute knowledge you are cannot be made more or less. That's the only quality of knowledge and not a quantity of, more, more, more insights, deeper, higher. That's all bullshit. That's all a quantity of shit. *chit* has no quantity, no size. You cannot find quantity of more or less in Knowledge. And that what is more or less, is shit. More or less shit, that's all. That's why shit happens. In *chit* nothing happens.

And I can just repeat it and repeat it and listen to it. It's an infinite talking to myself.

Q: So, when you say the whole movie is already there, are you talking about that block?

K: I am talking about the Absolute block of existence. If you call it a movie, every moment is a frame of existence. But these moments in nature, are absolute life itself. Life is not born in that moment and it cannot die in the next moment.

Q [Another visitor]: When you call it a block, it sounds like it has corners...

K: You can imagine it as whatever you like.

Q [Another visitor]: Even physicists are saying that the existence is a block...

K: They seem to be saying that there is no time involved in that. That in coming nothing comes. That energy is not created and it cannot be exhausted. So, there is never any exhaustion of energy or life. That what is the nature of energy can never be exhausted. It shows itself infinitely differently but it is never exhausted by showing itself. That's what they are concluding and I would say the same.

Life can never be exhausted by experiencing itself. It doesn't need any energy to experience itself. That's why you can call it a dream of experiences. In dream of experiences, you don't need energy to dream. The energy you are doesn't need energy to dream. It's just a natural inexhaustible life. That's why it's a block. Because in the block of no coming, no going, nothing happens. And when nothing happens, no energy is involved, no energy is needed. Energy is only needed in coming and going. If that really would happen, that something is exhausted in creating something or that in destroying it needs some extra energy. But if nothing is ever created and nothing will ever be destroyed, where is the exhaustion?

So, if they come now to the block theory, why not? Welcome! It will go again.

Q: So, the incident that happened yesterday, the blade runner killing his girlfriend, would it be considered as an extreme experience?

K: No. Only when you make a story out of it. For existence, it's the next sip of coffee; killing your girlfriend.

Q: Is that experience of killing extreme?

K: It's just bullshit. Everyone wants to be special; he wants a special story out of hell. And everyone wants to make his little story a special one.

Q: When you would hear this on news...

K: I would love. It's really funny. No one would really give a shit if it was another guy in South Africa. There would be no notice of it even in newspaper. But since this guy was running with his bloody blades, then the whole world gives attention to that. It's a joke. It happens in neighborhood slums every day. And the whole police doesn't care, they just send someone to pick up the body. But if it's some famous guy, everyone thinks – Did he really kill? Oh my goodness.

Q: Immaterial of whether it's a high profile killing, what's your personal advice in this situation?

K: Just get a good lawyer and see what happens. [Laughter] I would just be practical. Don't say anything, your lawyer will lie for you. He knows how to lie better than you, that's why they call him liar (lawyer). He is a professional liar, you still need to learn. So, if you have done something get a professional liar, the best you can get. The one who knows how to handle the other liars – the judges. [Laughter]

Q: If something like this happened to someone I know, my reaction would be – Oh no...

K: You would love it inside and pretend as if you are sorry.

Q: No...

K: Be honest.

Q: I am honest...

K: No. The one who says I am honest, for sure is not honest. It's like two girlfriends meeting and one is totally heartbroken and the other one is consoling... awww, poor you. Even when your husband died, you are like... awww, why didn't that happen to me? [Laughter] No one has compassion, I tell you.

Q: All these instances are already in the can?

K: Already happened, could not be avoided. It's impossible to avoid anything. In that way or this little way, no word that comes out of my mouth can be avoided. I cannot say one time less bitch than what I say. [Laughter] You cannot avoid the avoidance, avoidance will happen. Because the one who wants to avoid avoidance, is the biggest avoider.

Q: Can you say something on gratitude?

K: It's bullshit. The only gratitude you should have is that you don't need to have any gratitude to be what-you-are. The absolute gratitude that you don't need one.

Q: So, what is the overwhelming arising that happens?

K: It's an emotional overload. I am so fucking loaded. It's a sentimental journey that happens when you are loaded or overloaded. I would not know for what? It can only be a relative emotional something...

Q [Another visitor]: Ramana had an experience...

K: No. Now you make him a relative teacher, speaking out of experience.

Q: Is there any event?

K: You can call it a split second but you cannot put it in time. It's, by the way and not because-of something. I am not because the story went the way it did.

Q: It has to be. If I would have met you thirty years back, you would not have said what you are saying...

K: I would have talked about the Absolute as now.

Q: But you did not...

K: But if you would have met and asked me the question, I would have spoken as Absolute as now.

Q [Another visitor]: On the same subject?

K: On the same Absolute, the same solid block. For twelve years, when I was plowing the field sitting on a tractor and looking at one line for ten hours a day. I had so much time thinking about eternity. It really felt like eternity, ten hours a day looking at that line. So, I wanted to know what eternity was. Then for two weeks I was obsessed with the question, what is the meaning of eternity? Then I came to the point that, if I sit here again in whatever future and the field and every little soil are the same as it is right now. The same circumstance, all the satellites, the sun, all whatever is exactly the same. And if it is not exactly as it is, it would take another eternity to be the same. In eternity, everything will be exactly what is, as it is now.

So, it has already happened again and again. So, this moment is silence, it never comes, it never went. It is exactly as it is. There was no Karl anymore in that moment, there was just eternity. No coming, no going. That was the death experience. Death experience which means nothing comes, nothing goes, nothing is born and nothing dies. I was always pondering on eternity. It was like training. So, if you ask me, it was a long time ago. But not by reading books, it was just that the circumstance dictated this; putting me in that field and making me ponder about that line.

Q [Another visitor]: Is that what you call preparation?

K: That's what I call preparation that I can talk like I talk. But it doesn't make me more as I Am. Everything is preparation; milking cows, talking with a fascist from the village, being fearless of getting beaten up.

Q: So there is no less preparation here [Pointing to herself] as it is there [Pointing to Karl]?

K: No. You prepared your whole life just to have this question and sit on that corner as I am absolutely prepared to sit here and talk about what I talk about. It's all a preparation of a tool. But that what is your nature never needs to be prepared. But every little thing prepared you. Ramana said the same to a visitor. You took a ship, a train, a bullock cart to get here. But all of that had to happen so that you can sit here and have this experience.

Q: So, one could say that for Z to happen, A, B, C has to happen…

K: I would say – because the future is already as it is, the past has to be as the past is. So that I already had to sit here and talk like this, I had to have all the experiences that lead to this point. There is the same destiny of everyone who sits here that one day the body will die. That's the absolute destiny. So, it has already happened.

And all what you collected with this body, all of that will be gone and you have to be without it again. So, be now with it, what you will be without it – that's all. And you have nothing to gain in it because whatever you gain now in this body in one instant is gone. As every night, when you go in deep-deep sleep there is no one who remembers anything. There is no scientist, no enlightened one in deep-deep sleep. And the same will be the case when this body is gone, everything is gone – Pang! As if nothing ever happened.

So, be now what-you-are with the body as you were without.

Q [Another visitor]: But you say the birth and death is fixed…

K: I say the experience is fixed. There is an experience of birth but no one is born and there will be an experience of death but no one will die. As there's no one born in the first place, there will be no one who dies in the death experience. So, nothing ever happens by that.

You were, you are and you will be – what-you-are. And That does not have anything to gain here or to lose. You didn't gain a body and you cannot lose it. You never owned the body as what-you-are. You have nothing to lose here otherwise you cannot sleep at night anymore. You would be afraid that you could not wake up in the morning. Your precious little body would not be there anymore. You just fall in love with an imaginary piece of shit and now you are stuck in it.

Q [Another visitor]: So, love and stupidity are same?

K: Yes, my dear. [Laughter] Love really makes you stupid. What else can make you stupid to believe that you depend on – what you call this. It's an amazing force.

Q [Another visitor]: Are we a by-product of creation?

K: I would say we are a bye-bye product. [Laughter]

Q: What I mean is, is it garbage?

K: No, it's just one experience out of infinite experiences. I would even say, without you or any of your cells, the absolute would not be as the absolute is. The absolute can only be absolute because all whatever happened and not happened is as the absolute is. You cannot miss one little aspect out of it. I call it rubbish because you believe that you cannot be without it. Then it becomes rubbish.

Otherwise, it's just a next experience of … whatever. But you making your life depending on it, you make it rubbish. What is it? Just the next, the next, the next.

Q [Another visitor]: Would you say it's all an illusory experience experienced by an illusory experiencer?

K: One can say that, but who would understand that? You can say all is Lila.

Q: Is it the same idea for Maya?

K: Maya is the idea of time.

Q: The experiencer that's imagined…

K: That's the idea of time. Maya means that the experiencer is different from what is he is experiencing. It's a dream.

Q: But time is also an imaginary concept…

K: Yeah. That's part of Maya too. There is no Maya without time and there is no time without Maya. They are not two.

Q: Everything is imaginary…

K: But who says that?

Q: It is an existing theory…

K: Stay there. I don't want to employ another concept of Maya. I am not here to make a course for a scholar.

Q: It's not about being a scholar. One is just trying to understand...

K: But even that is too much. Trying to control is trying to understand, it's not different in nature.

Q: There is no question of controlling...

K: You want to control – believe it. Understanding is a tool of controlling. Trying to know is trying to control oneself – out of fear.

February 16, 2013
Mumbai, India

Chapter Nine

The Truth You Can Experience, Is A Fake Truth

Q: This year I have been losing a lot of relationships...

K: When you turn sixty you have to get rid of all the false apples.

Q: It has been a really hard year...

K: No. It is the best what you can get; losing all the fake friends.

Q: I don't know if they were fake...

K: Friends are always fake, that is not the question. You hold on to fake things a lot. Normally you get a cat when you turn sixty because then that's the only relationship you like.

Q: I put a lot of value to money and relationships and they both are just going away...

K: As long as you have something, it may go. But it sounds like you still have money. [Laughter] But you still wait for the complainer to go.

Q: That would be bliss...

K: And I sit here and tell you it will never go. It wakes up in the morning and goes to bed with you. Always waits on the bed before you wake up; waiting to talk to you.

Q: This time I felt that I wanted to be here. Most of the other times I had so much resistance...

K: For me too. [Laughter] I keep asking – Why the fuck am I going there? Why am I sitting here? They don't need me, I don't need them. It's maybe easier if you don't resist as you have to sit here anyway. Liking it or not is not the question, it will happen anyway. Resistance is futile.

Q [Another visitor]: But even that you cannot help...

K: No. Resistance drops when it drops not because you want it to drop.

Q [Another visitor]: And when does it drop?

K: It just drops but then it may come back. That what can go can come back again. You can never know, it's a surprise. But no one needs it to drop, that's the main thing. It drops and then it comes back. What to do? There was no disadvantage with resistance and there is no advantage without resistance. That's all. It doesn't make her more or less as she is – never was. It's just as if the movie continues with a different scenery; different emotions, different sensations. Differences after differences after differences. But they never make any difference for what-you-are. They have no consequences – never had. There will be the next, like the next sip of water.

Q [Another visitor]: The pain is there but after sometime it recedes to a distance...

K: But then you go back into it again. Sometimes you shift to the witness then you cannot feel it. You just witness the ones who feels the pain. But then suddenly you get involved again. Then it's back to torture. Sometimes it's like watching television and other times it's being totally involved in the program; out of the program, into the program.

But your existence was not different. As a witness you are not different to that what you are observing. You will always go back. You fall in love with the next – whatever. You are curious again what's happening there. Then you are back in business and then you feel the pain again.

Q: So, there's no advantage at all?

K: That's the beauty. How many times have I told you that – there is no advantage in being there and no disadvantage in being here. As there is no one who could have an advantage in one of those places. They are just different sensational experiences.

Q: The first verse of the book Echoes Of Silence says if grace is after you, then you cannot find satisfaction anywhere...

K: That you don't find any advantage in any place. And by not finding any advantage in any better place, the whole idea of advantage and disadvantage drops – just by being what-you-are. Because what-you-are never needs an advantage or disadvantage – never had one. There is no ownership in anything; no relative ownership.

You are That but it is not something you can gain or attain. By being what-you-are, you cannot gain or lose anything. You cannot be more or less as that what-is. So, what is there to do? And as you are That, you have to have the next experience of yourself. You cannot stop realizing yourself. Never ending story.

Everyone overlooks when reading Nisargadatta; he calls it the ocean of pain. The ocean of relative experiences are always painful and the experience of separation you cannot stop. There is no other way of experiencing yourself. There will always be an experience of two. It's a duet of one. The one has to always experience itself as two – no way out. Sometimes there is oneness and sometimes there is separation. Oneness is your preference and you try to avoid the rest. Being one with my beloved and then being separated again.

Q: And being prior?

K: Being prior is just trying to escape. It's another escape point. You think if I am established in the prior, there no one can touch me. When I am prior, I am out of it, I found a place where I am free of suffering. But who needs that? Being free of what?!

Q: ME...

K: Yeah, 'me' again. It's nice but thank God is not nice enough. And if you cannot be in any given circumstance what-you-are, what is worth being it? When I ask you to be laziness itself, just be lazy. But everyone told you laziness is best and I tell you it's the best you can be.

Your nature is being a lazy bastard; you know that. [Laughter] If you have a choice, you would never wake up from deep sleep. But now you are awake and now it's too late. Now things happen until they stop again; then they happen again. It's exhausting, but what to do? But your nature cannot be exhausted, that's the problem. The absolute problem that your nature cannot be exhausted. As much as you try to exhaust yourself – no way. Always fresh again, as it was before. Never gets tired by anything. No way to retire from all of that. So, you may retire from the idea of retirement. No way out!

This is what it means by 'when grace is after you', it shows no pity. If I would pity you, I would try to help you. I would show you techniques of how to get out of it. But from me you don't get any help, I tell you. No transmission of anything. No Shakti from this guy.

Q [Another visitor]: Nothing...

K: Nothing is too much. [Laughter]

Q [Another visitor]: But in the state of helplessness where you can't do anything, a constant tape goes on – should I do something or should I not do anything inspite of knowing the helplessness of the situation. But the conflict doesn't stop...

K: Why should it? What would you gain by stopping it?

Q: Some peace...

K: What kind of peace would that be? A relative peace which depends on something to stop. Who needs this relative peace? Only 'me'. Even succeeding in something makes it stronger. Even succeeding is worse. Making it work is the worst what could happen because you think you can do something. That by whatever you have done, whatever you have understood, you can enter some peace. Even that is a misunderstanding. Every understanding, whatever you do or don't do, whatever level you reach is a relative peace – fleeting, coming going, or not...

The main question is who has the advantage? Who needs it? And the answer is always 'me'. That what-you-are never needs anything; it is absolutely satisfied by being what-it-is. And that what you experience is always needy. The body needs to breathe, the mind needs to think. All what you can name or frame needs something.

Q: That's what you mean when you say be the laziest?

K: The laziest never did anything. There is no doership. That's what Ramesh called absolute non-doership for what-you-are. It never has done anything, never even woke up, never goes to bed. Even the slightest thing is never done by that what-you-are. There is absolute non-doership by that what is existence because this is never happening. There is no happening. Nothing is ever created, never can be destroyed. It was always as it is – a block of existence.

Every moment, every frame is never coming, never going. So, nothing is ever done. No creation, no destruction. As nothing was ever created, nothing can be destroyed. Shiva is destroying the idea of destruction. That is the real meaning of destroying – the idea that you can destroy something. That something has to go or to come 'to be'. So, the real chopping of the head is that no one needs to chop your head. That no one needs you to be different – with or without. No one cares! Life is living you as you are and never cares about how it is. It's always as it is and not because you have a different understanding – it starts liking you more. It doesn't even know you.

Q [Another visitor]: But why does this continuous 'tape' overrule the basic nature of life?

K: There is no basic nature of life. What would be the basic nature and what would not be the basic nature? Already that is an idea. Life is not an idea. But if you make it a basic nature, then you already make it a concept.

You can say your natural state is absolutely not knowing what-you-are and what-you-are-not. The absolute absence of whatever one knows what one is. That would be your basic nature. That is what-you-are here now. It's not something new. It is not something that comes by understanding. The knowledge 'you are' is independent of a knower who knows or doesn't know anything. That you have never lost so you cannot gain it back by this way of understanding. Whatever understanding happens now never adds to your basic nature which is knowledge. It doesn't take anything away nor does it give anything. So, what to do?

Try your best but it's never good enough. Still you have to try. Inquiry will never stop; no way of stopping it. The lover loving the beloved is trying to know himself infinitely; in his infinite story of the love affair with himself. In a passionate love with itself; drama after drama. When there is Rama there is drama, I tell you.

When Rama knows Rama, then he starts his drama because then he falls in love with an image of himself. Then he tries to do the best out of it but it will never be good enough. So, it's a long way back home because you never left home. So, it's a very long way home – unreachable. If you really would have left home, there would be a way home. One day sooner or later you would reach it again. But as you never left, no way home. It's a joke from the beginning. And I sit here and tell this to whom? [Laughter]

I should be complaining, I tried telling this to myself for so many years but it's a never ending story. I have to sing the song which no one needs. Singing, singing, singing; doing my best but it's never good enough. And I should be happy that it's never good enough because if one thing I say would be good enough, it could be spoken, it could be pronounced and someone could understand it – that would be really bad. That someone would get something out of it; even the idea itself is bad.

Nothing happens, no one gets it, no one needs it – fantastic! And still it goes on.

Q [Another visitor]: You said that there is no creation no destruction. I am having a hard time with that...

K: If you see that nothing happened; that in coming nothing comes and in going nothing goes, then there would be no hard time anymore because then there is no time. But now you want to solve the problem which was never there. You can say the mind creates the problem which would not be there without the mind. He makes sure that there would be problems which you ponder about it because without it he would kill himself and he would never do that. Something wrong? That's the mind. The control system getting triggered.

It's fantastic. This program of caring never stops – that's love, loving caring about what goes on. Defending what can be defended, building armours around. All the tendencies in this universe are love tendencies. Then there is war about 'me' and 'you'. Never stops.

Nothing ever happens means out of absolute light, absolute potential, it realizes itself moment-by-moment. And in coming nothing comes and in going nothing goes. That would be the end of your little 'me' because it lives by the idea that in coming something comes and by going something goes. Without the story of something coming and going, there is no 'me'; never was.

In that sense, I am pointing out that I cannot make it true for you. But just by being what-you-are, 'this' is. That's why they call it silence, the peace of 'what is'. That there is no coming and no going in it and there no one to find something else. But still the movie goes on 'as if'. The experience tells you that there's something coming but it's a false experience – coming and going. Then you fear that you lose something and you fear that you gain in something coming. But it is a false evidence appearing real; that is fear.

You say I have a body; you need evidence all the time that you exist. Fantastic! That's called 'me'; always needs proof. Because it's so fleeting, this phantom 'me'. It has no substance at all; it does not have any reality. It needs moment-by-moment a proof of its existence. And problems are the best proof that 'it is' – having or not having, enough or not enough all of that. Bastard!

Q: It's hard not to get trapped in that...

K: You cannot stop it. That's the nature of the phantom, what can you do? It is fighting for life. The unreal wants to become real; it will never stop trying to become real. That's the nature of unreal; trying moment-by-moment to become real. It always needs proof of what-it-is; proving and improving. [Laughter]

And you have to be inspite of it; you cannot kill it because that is consciousness. Consciousness already is fake existence – false. And the false needs to prove itself. Inquiring into its nature, inquiring and proving and improving, transmuting into a higher consciousness – higher higher higher, lower lower lower, deeper deeper deeper. [Mocking] I want to be high; stoned forever. [Laughter]

Then it gets addicted to understanding because understanding gives him the proof of existence. I understand, so I have to be of high intelligence. Then you make a claim about what-you-are. First you claim that you are the body, then you claim I am the spirit, then you claim the awareness. If that is not enough, I claim to be prior. I get established in prior; but at least I have something to claim. I know I am prior. But who is that bastard who knows that he is the prior? For what? Then you have a prayer – please let me be the prior. Then the 'prior' religion starts.

I joke about everything because that is what I Am. I realize myself as a stupid guy. Dream realizing itself in ignorance, realizing myself as false trying to become real. It's fun. It's a fun-tom (phantom) but sometime it becomes a sad-tom.

Q [Another visitor]: So, what is it that is real?

K: I have no idea. [Laughter] You can say that 'what is', is not an idea. But that you cannot know. Whatever you know, especially the knower is a concept, the knowing is a concept and what can be known is a concept. But that there can be a concept of a knower, knowing, what can be known, there has to be what-you-are. That there can be a presence of knower, knowing, what can be known, what-you-are has to be with and without it.

So, pre-sense you can say is Reality. That what is in-no-sense and with-sense.

Q: From where does that Reality come?

K: How can it come? That what never comes in coming and never goes in going, that you can call Reality. And the concept which comes and goes for sure is not Reality. And I say that is what you are because in coming you don't come and in going you don't go. So, in birth you are not born and in dying you don't die.

That what-you-are already had to be there before perception could happen before the two liquids meet. For all of that what-you-are had to be. Before even the experience of being can happen, you have 'to be'. That you can call Reality but even calling it Reality is too much. You better don't know what-you-are and what-you-are-not.

Q: So all this is happening naturally?

K: I don't say anything about that. I just say this is as it is. It cannot be different because it is as it is. Then the next will be different but it is still what-it-is.

Q: I don't have to put any effort for it to come...

K: You don't have to put any effort for the next sensation to come because the next sensation is already there, you don't have to create it. It's a natural experience. It's a natural realization of what-you-are. But they are all lies, they are real lies. All what you can experience, the experiencer, the experience, what can be experienced, are real lies. That's why it's called real-lie-zation. Reality realizing itself in lies, in false evidence, false sensations. Even calling it false is false because only the false says something is false.

Q: But at this moment this is what I understand...

K: And the next moment you understand something else. So, just enjoy it because it wouldn't last. And you don't need it. That's the beauty of it that you don't need to understand to be what you are. So, if you understand that I don't need to understand to be what I am, even that understanding comes and goes. You never needed anything.

Q: So, I don't put any effort, the thought comes to me, the sensation comes to me?

K: As I said, you are the laziest bastard you cannot know. You cannot know the lazy bastard you are, but you are That. So, whatever you know is not what-you-are. So, be the laziness that never needs to know itself.

Q: From where does 'what you are' come?

K: It never came, how can it come? To who? before coming, 'you are' and before going 'you are' and after going 'you are'. You are before, now and beyond.

Q: But we use the perception that we have...

K: You are the perception, perception perceiving the perceiver. But the perceiver is already perceived by what-you-are. You are the absolute experiencer experiencing the experiencer. But that what is experiencing the experiencer cannot experience itself. So, the experiencer already is an experience. The knower is something what you know. But that what knows the knower, you cannot know. And that what is the knower in essence, which is with and without the knower experience never needs the knower to know more or less to be what-it-is; inspite of the presence of the knower or the absence of the knower. That you call knowledge – *sat-chit-ananda*. That what is ananda never needs to experience ananda. The joy never needs to enjoy itself. The peace that never can be destroyed by something else because there is nothing what is second to that.

Q: But still I experience the destruction...

K: The peace has to experience itself as war because whatever you can experience is war. Peace can never be experienced. The peace you can experience is a fake one. The fake peace you can experience, you have to fight for it. The truth you can experience is a fake truth. And the fake truth, you fight for. Like religion. The God you can know – my God – you fight for that God. The God you don't know, you cannot fight for. So, everyone fights for peace, for an idea.

Q: I just understand that I am alive, the experiences come to me and I am suffering. I cannot understand that I am That...

K: No. What-you-are never suffered. When you wake up in the morning, the sufferer wakes up and then the suffering starts. Then in the night, the sufferer drops but you are with and without the sufferer. So, you cannot say you are suffering. You are uninterrupted. You have an experience of a sufferer or suffering or doing something. But it doesn't make you a sufferer.

Q: But with my mind, this is all that I can understand...

K: The mind will always be limited by relative understanding. So, whatever can be understood is a relative understanding. It doesn't matter how deep it goes, how high it goes, how intelligent one is, it's all limited. You will never reach the end of knowledge. So, crazy wisdom is the wisdom that doesn't know any wisdom because there is no one who is wise. You don't even know what is and what is not wisdom. That's called the nature of knowledge, where no one knows any beginning or end of anything as there is no knower. That knowledge never comes or goes by anything. It does not depend on any insights or outsides, as knowledge has no inside or no outside; no quantity of more or less to it.

All these pointers pointing to that what-you-are which you never lost. So, you cannot gain it back by anything. So, whatever you gain now, is fake – just bullshit. Because only shit can be gained. But *chit* can never be gained. As it cannot be gained, it cannot be attained. As you have never lost it, you cannot get it back and whatever you get now is coming, going, fleeting. Forget it!

Enjoy it as long as it lasts, I would say. And you cannot stop it, the next comes anyway. As the last went, the next comes. Tick-tock-tick-tock, like time. I can just point to that, I cannot help you. And you don't need any help by anyone. You are already the almighty itself – the almighty energy. But you have to experience yourself as an impotent bastard. Fantastic!

You are the omnipotent God – God himself, the Absolute. But you can only experience yourself as an impotent 'me' as you can never experience yourself as that what-you-are. You realize yourself as a little impotent bastard. So, what? Does it make you impotent by experiencing yourself as impotent? No! Your omnipotence of the life you are was never lost. Now experiencing yourself as a little Shiva, a *jiva* doesn't make Shiva a *jiva*. Shiva is still Shiva experiencing itself as a *jiva*. So, no problem. There was never any problem.

Q: The absolute can never be known. So, how did it come into existence? How are we talking about it?

K: You talk about that which doesn't exist.

Q: So, it is a concept...

K: Yes. Now we talk of concepts, pointers. What-you-are, the Absolute doesn't even need a concept of absolute. It doesn't even need the word absolute.

Q: But there is no way of knowing that I am the Absolute...

K: No. But still you are that.

Q: So, how can I take the position that I am the Absolute suffering as a small me?

K: That's what I am asking how can you do that? But look you did it. [Laughter] How can you do that? It's amazing. I am totally amazed by myself that the absolute you-are takes the position of a little suffering bastard. Look how it happens everywhere. Seven billion little absolutes believing that they are born. How can that happen? I am totally amazed by myself. How absolute stupid can it be?

For me it is fantastic. As the absolute knowledge, it can be absolute stupid. It never loses its absolute nature. So, if it's absolute knowledge – fantastic. If it's absolute stupid, it's absolute stupid. It absolutely knows by being what-it-is and it absolutely doesn't know when it believes in being born.

Shiva starting a puppet house became his own puppet. Fantastic! How can that happen? And nothing happens. It's a mystery in a way. Ramana would say how can the Self look for the Self? It never lost itself. How can the absolute self start looking for the Self? No one can ever explain why? I would say why not? Does it matter? Having a little dance with yourself. Falling in love with your little image. Does it make you less? No. Does it make you more? No. So, no problem.

But as you started to realize yourself as what-you-are, there is one part which is heaven, pleasure, and there is other part which is pain, hell. And you can only experience yourself in both absolute parts. You cannot only have one part of knowing. With knowing comes ignorance too. There is darkness and light. All of that has to be. And you cannot choose between that, you are That.

Buddha said the divine accident happened. The divine woke up and now since it's awake, it has to realize itself. Like it or not. But it cannot realize itself only in one possible way. It has to realize itself in all the possible ways. And one possible way is being a human, waking up in the morning and questioning – Who Am I? What am I doing here? What is the purpose of life? All those things have to happen if you ask me. But it's not needed even to understand that.

I just point to it. For me, the absolute potential has to realize itself in every possible way.

Q: So, nothing is left out?

K: No. The Taoists would say you cannot take one sensation out of totality. If you could take one sensation out, totality would not be total any more. Totality has to be total realizing totally in whatever can happen or not. It cannot take one thing out of it.

Q: You have to take the whole bag...

K: Yeah. The quantum theorists would say if you could take one particle out of the universe, the whole universe would not exist. It has to be as it is. Absolutely total in itself and part of it is being a bloody human and questioning what one is; as bad as it is. I think being human is the worst. Nothing is worse than being a human.

Q: Do you think inanimate things like table also go through this cycle?

K: No. The table does not know it's a table, so the table doesn't care. Only the humans care whether the table cares or not. [Laughter] The table knows more than us. It gives a shit if it's a table or not. Your little finger knows more than you. Ask your finger, how are you today? Silence. No one talks to you. Then you go back to the place where there is a loudspeaker and microphone inside and start the mind-fuck inside, how are you today? It's very intimate, this mind-fuck. It never stops. But what else can the mind do? A little bit of sex is not so bad. Be generous.

Q: Mind never gets realized?

K: No.

Q: So, it never stops?

K: It never slows down. Experience of separation – that is called as mind. You can only experience yourself in two. There is an experiencer experiencing what can be experienced. There is always an experiencer of a lover and a beloved. The lover will always want to know, who is that what I see? The experiencer wants to know what is he seeing. He wants to control it. It's like a snake looking at its own tail and experiencing the tail as a second snake.

Q: What does UG mean by the mind falling in a natural rhythm?

K: By being the snake but not knowing any snake. That's your natural state.

Q: What happens at that point? Does the mind slow down?

K: There is no time any more. That's why it's called the split second. You split the idea of a second by being what-you-are in a split second. Just by splitting the idea of second, there was never any mind because mind never minds mind. At first there is mind and no mind. You mind the no mind. The mind wants to be the no mind, by stopping the mind. But as long as the mind wants to stop the mind, there is a mind trying to stop the mind. Infinite slavery.

So, in one split second, by being the mind you don't know what is mind anymore. That is falling in the mind by being the mind. That's the natural state. That is total resignation on resigning. But it cannot be done, that's the problem. Whatever you do is counter-productive. But still you have the tendency of not having the tendency. You still have the tendency that no-mind is better than the mind. That keeps the mind minding the mind.

Q: So, utter helplessness will never happen?

K: No. In helplessness there is no time. Time is only when there is help or no help. In helplessness, nothing ever happened. There is nothing to stop because nothing ever happened there. Only when there is two, mind and no mind, then there is time, there are differences. In the timelessness of existence, what can happen? There is peace – always was, always will be. Then the peace has a little restlessness and then it starts to realize itself in one and the other. Oneness-separation, oneness-separation; all those differences. Never ending story.

They all are because 'you are'. And because you are That, this is the way you experience yourself. And no end; no way out of it. Even for UG, there was no way out. That's why he always called it, no way out. You never went in, how can you get out? Now we hope for no-hope. No. It will never be good enough.

Q: So, all the spiritual traditions are a big joke?

K: You are a joke. We are all jokes, like little farts of existence. We smell for a while and then we are gone; like every religion. Imagine in a hundred thousand years would anyone remember that there was a Christ who was crucified? Hundred thousand years is just a blink of an eye for *Parabrahman*. But do you think in a hundred thousand years anyone would remember a guy being crucified if there are no humans left to remember. But existence will still be what-it-is.

So, with and without humanity and all the problems that came along with it, existence will be there. Maybe in infinity there again will be another humanity. This moment would repeat itself, because it was not gone. Then we sit here and talk about the same problem which was never there. [Laughter]

And you still will be what-you-are, you were, you are, you will be – with and without these problems of humanity. And the problems will come back again as you cannot escape them. Next time you will be as stupid as you are now. But does it make you stupid? No. You just experience yourself as stupid but that doesn't make you stupid like experiencing yourself now as human doesn't make you human. That I can only point to. And I have to listen to that for a long time, what this guy [Referring to himself] says.

Q [Another visitor]: Human beings are big garbage...

K: A compost, decomposed already. Whatever you see now is already decomposed. This is already gone – wrinkled or not. Every morning you look in the mirror and say – With me the wrinkles would be gone too, don't worry. A piece of meat getting wrinkled.

Q: Even if there is no creation and no destruction, human beings are garbage...

K: You cannot get rid of it because it never came and it can never go. It doesn't even exist now. How can you get rid of humanity that doesn't even exist now? That's the whole problem. You cannot even destroy something what is not there. How can you destroy ignorance? There was never any ignorance. There is only knowledge, there is only Self; call it whatever. Call it Absolute, call it existence, there is nothing but That. Presenting itself as whatever doesn't make it the way it presents itself. Seven billion non-existences walking... and counting. Having a family, what a joke! You believe you have parents and they believe that you are their child.

Q [Another visitor]: Your message of feeling hopeless resonates with my personal experience...

K: I don't say anything new. Everyone knows by heart what I say. It's not that I tell you something you don't know. This is the knowledge which was, is and will be what-you-are and is not something new that I can bring to you. It's not something that I found out and I can teach you something what you don't have.

No. This you don't need to learn. This is a natural knowledge. I am here more for taking away what you don't need, if at all. But I cannot take anything away either. I am the most useless guy I ever experienced. This total irrelevance of existence, that I like most. Absolute irrelevant – not good or bad for anything. That's not so bad, neither being good or bad for anything. Absolute irrelevant for existence. Doesn't bring anything, doesn't take anything away. If you call that peace, I would agree. It's quite peaceful, being a fool for oneself. So, peace-off and be the fool.

Q [Another visitor]: I don't know what I want and I am kind of happy to let go...

K: You are happy until you get it. The moment you got it, it makes you unhappy. I always tell people imagine you could know yourself. That would be hell. Even to imagine that you can know yourself, that's hell. That's the basis of suffering. Just an imagination that you could know yourself makes you two. How powerful this imagination is! As powerful as you imagining that you can be known. Any moment you imagine, you become an object of what can be known. Wow!

And I sit here and tell you; thank God you will never get it. So, be happy there is nothing to get.

Q [Another visitor]: There are people who say they have achieved maximum in life and the next moment they have suicidal tendencies...

K: The moment you know something, you have to lose it again, that's the punishment. The moment you claim that you got something, you are punished that you can lose it again. So, the fear is underlying everything. Having or not having – fear. Having too much or too less – fear. Fear, fear, fear. Never good enough. Ownership is fear and ownership is having or not having, always fear.

Q [Another visitor]: That goes with awareness as well...

K: Having or not having. Being or not being aware. It's the same. You are fucked the moment you have something.

Q: But I can't help it, I go back to trying to have more insights...

K: The greediness never stops.

Q: There is an obsession to know what's more...

K: You are totally obsessed with yourself. You want to know yourself; you want to be more aware, deeper and deeper. It's a joke. Enjoy the ride because you cannot stop it. Even by trying to stop the ride, you want to control yourself. You want to have yourself – totally; only you, no one else should have it. My beloved, I want to have you totally and I want to control you by that because I fear that you may otherwise do something I don't like. So, I better control you. My precious, like in The Lord Of The Rings. Then it eats you up inside out.

With love comes fear..... crazy! And you can't stop falling in love again. This is the most stupid thing, falling in love with what-you-are. Falling in love makes you two, and you cannot stop it. This love affair is infinite, never started and will never stop. The moment you wake up and awareness is there, there is a love affair. There is two – already. The most basic experience of awareness already is an experience of separation. Fantastic!

So, you are fucked from the beginning. And you are the fucker, the fucking and the fucked; whether you like it or not. Trying not to fuck yourself is the biggest fuck. Trying to establish yourself in a no-place where there is no-fucker and no-fucking is the biggest fuck. No way out. You will always try to penetrate yourself in every possible way, if you like it or not. This lingam is it's fucking nature. The lingam penetrates the space and creates the whole universe because by vibrating in space it creates all the differences of vibrations. As it cannot vibrate only in one way, it has to vibrate in all possible ways.

Adam the lingam and Eve the space vibrating in every possible way. They cannot just vibrate in a peaceful way. [Laughter] You cannot vibrate in only one possible way, but you have this preference. You want to be in peace with yourself and for that you fight. As you fight for peace, you create the other side too. You meditate for it – shamelessly. You want to go deep into your nature by meditating deeper and deeper and deeper.

Q: So, there's nothing really to it?

K: You cannot stop it. For stopping yourself, it needs two and there are no two, that's the whole problem. Only when there would be reality in two, there could be control, one who could control the other. But there are no two. You are That which creates one and two. Then not just this cannot control that, even That cannot control that. There is no control in anything.

In *Mahabharata* Krishna says, me as the architect of manifestation, I wrote the script perfectly when I woke up. But now I am totally helpless to change one little aspect of it. Even if I try to stop this war, I cannot. Total helplessness. It's already done.

What can I do? That's the best. How can I change what is already done? The movie is already shot, frame-by-frame.

Q [Another visitor]: Did Krishna ever experience that helplessness?

K: Yes, that is his pointer. Being in the world and cannot change any moment. You are Krishna, the Almighty who wrote the whole script of the whole manifestation, being potential of everything. And now you experience yourself being in the movie and you cannot change the movie. You cannot even change experiencing yourself being in the movie. Fantastic!

Moment-by-moment is an experience of helplessness. The almighty experiencing itself impotent of trying to change anything. Then we as humans believe that we can do something. If the Almighty itself cannot do anything, if the omnipotence itself cannot change anything, who do you pray to? If there really would be a God in its omnipotence and if even he cannot change his creation, what is there to pray to? If there really would be a God in God's will, even he cannot change what he wants. So, enjoy yourself as there is no other self to enjoy. And it will take a while, an infinite while. And if you don't enjoy yourself, there is no other self who enjoys you.

In the first hour itself I try to kill the questions and the questioner. Then I complain that there are no questions left.

Q [Another visitor]: What is happiness?

K: An idea. You should be happy that you don't have to be happy to be what-you-are because that's the nature of happiness. It doesn't need to know what-is and what-is-not happiness. That's called happiness. The rest is just an emotional bullshit. The noumenon does not need to know itself as there is no two. But the moment there is a happy and an unhappy 'me', then you want to know what is happiness. How can I get it? Where can I buy it? Then you go to the next shopping mall and have little experiences of orgastic fair-trade. You give money, you get something. There is a moment of peace.

Then you want it again and again, this moment of peace. For that you go shopping. Because the moment after it, you are dissatisfied again. These are the new churches, the temples of America around the world – the shopping malls of little ecstatic fair-trades of harmony. It's like a whore house. Even in temples, if you make a little puja, you get a little harmony. It's all about oneness. Like sex, you have an orgasm and there is a little moment of 'no me' and then you want to have it again.

That's why you have so many people around now. Creating a little 'me' just out of this tendency to have a 'no me'. Nature is quite tricky. Or there is a little moment of understanding where there is complete peace. Then after a moment you question again what you understood before. The questioning starts right after what you understood. When you understand it, you think that is clarity itself but the immediate next moment you question that clarity. Because you want to own it, you want to stay in it. By trying to own it, it's already spoiled.

The same goes for enlightenment. There is a moment of perfect peace and the moment afterwards you want to own it as 'my' enlightenment and then it's gone. Then you say next time I would not want it, I would just be quiet. Ha, Ha, Ha... The moment when you have it, it is so precious that you want to extend it forever. This little peace you want to have eternally. How stupid can it get? There is no beginning and no end of stupidity; as knowledge has no beginning and no end. You have to experience yourself in stupidity.

Q: So, happiness is an idea and sadness is also an idea?

K: It can only exist in opposites. You exist because there is unhappiness. Knowledge can only exist because there is ignorance. Whatever you name exists because it has an opposite. But what-you-are is inspite of it and that would never call itself anything. It doesn't call itself as Absolute or Knowledge or anything. It would never give itself a name as there is no one who defines itself. Without a definer, there is no definition. But the moment the definer wakes up, he wants to define himself. He always wants to get finer and finer and finer. No way out!

Q [Another visitor]: Does this also happen to a new-born baby?

K: Yeah, it wants to be happy. Sucking the breast is the normal tendency of getting in harmony. Trying to avoid pain in the stomach is a natural tendency. It never stops. In the brain too, it wants harmony by having some understanding. It is all a natural tendency for peace. Every tendency is for harmony.

Q: Is it not something we pick up through all these years?

K: No. It's there from the beginning. It never started, it was always there. The moment God knows God, there are two Gods and when there are two Gods he wants to get rid of at least one God. But God trying to get rid of God, he will always be two. When there are two Gods, there is already discomfort – the discomfort of two; from the beginning. For any experience, it needs two. God experiencing God is already two Gods. And no way out, that's the way it is.

Q: Do you think Christ or Krishna got away with it?

K: No. They are as real as you are. You can question, is Krishna real? Is there a name Krishna because I call him Krishna? Is there any Krishna in deep-deep sleep as there is no me? No. So, Krishna is only there when I am here. Then there is Krishna, Shiva, all the Gods, the entire universe. Is there a Krishna and all the Gods when I am in deep-deep sleep, as I am not there. No. They are as real as I am. They only exist in this dream of myself.

Q: Why don't we all terminate ourselves?

K: Many tried. But did something change? How many people commit suicide and go to war and get killed? They have the intention of ending something. Did it end? Look at it. Did something end by Christ being crucified? By all the understanding of all the sages of all times. By UG Krishnamurti, by Ramana, by all of that, did anything change? Is anything different in this so-called reality of human life? Is there more peace on earth? Absolutely not. Nothing changed.

So it seems like life is living itself and it continues that way infinitely. Inspite of all the sages, inspite of all these ideas, inspite of Nisargadatta or Ranjit or anyone. But they all pointed to it. What you see as Maharaj now is a dream object. And that what is the nature of Maharaj, can never be experienced, it never came and it will never go. People asked Ramana where would you go when you die? Ramana said, where can I go? I am That. Do you think when the body goes, I go? I didn't come with the body and I don't go with the body. Even the understanding that comes is fleeting, as the body is fleeting. It makes no difference.

Q: Did the same thing happen to Ramana? When in the morning he woke up, was he as stupid as me?

K: We have to ask Ramana.

Q: Is the knower of Absolute as stupid as everyone else when he wakes up in the morning?

K: Yes. How can he not? That's the nature of man; experiencing itself as being stupid. You can never experience knowledge, as you can never experience yourself as there are no two. Whatever you experience is separation and separation is false. Falsity can be experienced. Even Ramana experiencing himself is falsity. There is no way out. But still he would say you have to realize yourself. As you are That in deep-deep sleep what-you-are, you are now what-you-are. And as you are now what-you-are, this is your realization.

You are the Absolute dreamer dreaming the dreamer and the dream. But you are with and without it, that's all. You are not because of the dream. Your nature has no cause, but you are the cause of all and you cannot stop it. *Parabrahman* as the absolute dreamer starts to dream, he dreams himself as the dreamer dreaming what can be dreamt. Now the dreamer believes that the dreamer is different to what he is dreaming. That creates the belief system that I am different to what I see. That's 'me', that's ignorance.

You are That what is realizing itself as the dreamer, dreaming, what can be dreamt. That's your natural state. Not knowing what-you-are and what-you-are-not. You absolutely don't know what-you-are and what-you-are-not. And by that you are the dreamer, dreaming, what can be dreamt; and you are not that. You are neither that (dreaming) or that (not dreaming) by not knowing what-you-are or what-you-are-not. Because there is no one who defines himself as that or that. That is you in deep-deep sleep and that is what-you-are now, as that is not different.

Your nature in deep-deep sleep is as absolute as it is, as it is now what-it-is. So, to know yourself as you know yourself in deep-deep sleep is being what-you-are now as you are in deep-deep sleep. And that never knows what-it-is and what-it-is-not. And that what you experience now, who claims to have a body, is a fleeting experience of a 'me' who identifies himself as something. But where is this 'me' in deep-deep sleep? But still you-are. So, you are with and without the little 'me'. That phantom you cannot get rid of. It will be there waiting for you and it will be gone when you are not.

By your experiencing, it's there and by your not experiencing it, it's gone. So, you are not depending on it, that's all. But still you cannot get rid of it. What to do? The phantom cannot be killed. If it would exist, you could kill it. If there would be any reality in 'me', you could get rid of it. But you try to get rid of the phantom which doesn't even exist. So, how to destroy the dream? And who needs to destroy it? That's the main question. Who would be better off without the dream?

The answer is instantly 'me'. But the 'me' is only there when experiences are. But you are not depending on them, as you are with and without the experience. So, know yourself as That, there is nothing more to it. And this will always fish in the dark here. The 'me' wakes up in the morning like a fisherman wanting to fish for some bigger fish; never satisfied with how big the fish is. Then he wants to sell the fish he catches – that's called selfish. Selling the fish and that stinks from the beginning. Selling the fish from the sea of ignorance. You can only fish what comes out of the sea of ignorance. It stinks from the beginning and by instinct you should know that.

Q [Another visitor]: In *Bhagavad Gita* Krishna says when everyone sleeps, the yogi does not sleep. What does that mean?

K: It means what-you-are never woke up so it cannot go to sleep. A *jñani* doesn't know any *jñani* and that what is *jñana* doesn't know any *jñana*. And by not knowing whether it is awake or not-awake, it is neither awake nor not awake. It needs one who defines himself, being awake or not awake. And without that definer, where is awakeness and where is sleep? Does life ever sleep or wake up? The nature of what-you-are which is life itself never wakes up and never goes to sleep. So, there is not even a dream of life.

Q [Another visitor]: This dream is a big problem...

K: There are only problems in dream. So, the dream is a big problem. Then you want to solve problems which are in the dream.

Q: How not to dream?

K: That is part of the dream.

Q [Another visitor]: You mean life is dreaming that we are talking to Karl?

K: Life is living life by what we are just doing. This is life being alive.

Q: But is it also a dream?

K: Life would not care if it is dream or not. Life doesn't know life, so it doesn't care if it's dream or not a dream. So, live your life as life lives you anyway. Live your life as life lives you because there is no difference. That's all. Life is living life.

Q: Does this mean that you are as stupid as we are?

K: I am stupidity itself. [Laughter] No one is more or less stupid than me. If there is an idea of stupidity, I am that. That is – I Am That. What is not me? As I don't know what is 'me', I don't know what is not 'me'. I don't know what I am and I don't know what I am not. That's your natural state. That would be knowledge which doesn't know what-it-is and what-it-is-not. But the moment you know yourself, you are fucked.

Q: So, the 'I don't know' situation is the best?

K: Then you still know too much. [Laughter] It sounds good – I know that I don't know. But there's still one-too-many who knows that he doesn't know. He is still part of, call it whatever. It's part of the dream. That's the beauty of what-you-are. You will never know what-you-are. You can name it whatever, it doesn't mind. That's the beauty, it never minds. You can even call it underwear, call it shit. It never minds, never reacts. You can call it sun or call it a cunt. It never minds.

It is the action but what you can experience is only reaction. But the action cannot be experienced. Energy cannot be experienced by energy. So, energy has to experience itself as a reaction of energy. This is a reaction of your existence. This is a reaction, but not the action. You can never experience yourself as action. You can only experience yourself as a reaction. Reaction means actor acting what can be acted. The creator, creating, what can be created. But the creator is a reaction of your existence.

God experiencing himself as a creator already is a second-hand experience; never first-hand. So, even the creator is a dream, creating is a dream, the creation is a dream. Fantastic! A big fantasy about yourself. And nothing to gain in it, that's the beauty. Nothing to gain, nothing to lose, by whatever that happens now or what happened before. It didn't make you less. And whatever would happen in future doesn't make you less or more as you are. That's the beauty. Nothing to lose in it, nothing to gain. You are absolute as you are in whatever that happens and did happen and will happen in whatever you can imagine. No imaginary circumstance, no imaginary dream can touch you or make you more or less as you are. Fantastic!

Where is the fear? You can only fear when you think it can make you less or you don't have enough. But you are not a quantity of anything. You are the quality of life and the quality cannot get more or less. Only quantity of bullshit can get more or less. That's why what is more or less is called shit; money or experiences or insights. Whatever you can count is not that what counts. That what counts, counts the counter counting what can be counted. Because it is the origin of the counter, counting, what can be counted. But it can never be part of the counting.

And that's the only thing what counts. You are the only thing what counts; existence itself, and not that what can be counted. So, you never came out of a cunt. [Laughter]

Q [Another visitor]: If there is no creation, no destruction, no me, no you, then why us?

K: There is but there is not. You cannot say there is not. There is, as an experience but that experience is an experience but not real. If it would be real, you would be born by being born and you could die. But you as what-you-are are not born in being born, you cannot die. But still you experience yourself as being born and you will experience death. But that you can experience death, you still have to be there experiencing death. So, death cannot touch you. As you are not born by being born, you cannot die in death.

So, birth doesn't make you born and death doesn't make you dead – that's all. All of that happens. But by none of those happenings, did something happen to you. That's all. I don't deny the happenings. But I deny that the happenings can do something to you or can make you more or less as you are. I don't deny anything of the dream. All of those are happenings of existence. But by none of those happenings, existence has something to gain or to lose anything.

So, your existence is as absolute as it can be. It cannot get more absolute or less absolute. That's why absolute is a pointer to what-you-are which can never be less or more. That's the quality of life.

Your nature is life itself which never needs to know life to be life. That's all. You don't own anything; you are That. Whatever you can name, you are. Whatever you cannot name, you are – in essence. And you have nothing to gain by anything.

And as you are knowledge, you cannot gain anything by any little understanding or you can lose anything by any misunderstanding. It's all fun. It's all just-in-case.

Q: Why are there so many contradictions?

K: You experience yourself in contradictions. How else can you experience yourself? You can only experience yourself as good or bad, by contradicting yourself. Even to say something is good is a contradiction. The moment you pronounce something, you contradict yourself. What else can you do? Whatever statement you make, it's questionable. Then you make another statement that contradicts the other one. So, what? If you can never say the truth, who gives a shit? Who cares what you say?

If what-you-are can never be pronounced, if it can never get more or less by what you say and what you do not, who fucking cares? That's all. You can be as silly, as you can be or you talk the golden wisdom. It does not make you more or less, so what? You can be extremely stupid but it doesn't make you stupid or you can be an Einstein but it doesn't make you more. So, fuck it all. Be the Einstein when you are the Einstein and be the idiot of the mad-house when you are the idiot of the mad-house.

If all of that doesn't make you or un-make you, so what? What is there to do, or not to do? All the doings, all the happenings, never did anything to you. And I can just repeat what Nisargadatta or Ranjit said. And it doesn't make any difference. That's what I like. This absolute irrelevance of what you say or what you don't say. If I tell it to you or not, it doesn't make you more or less. So, I don't need you and you don't need me. This is just a fun talk because we cannot otherwise. It happens anyway. So, we rather enjoy.

Thank God I cannot give you anything, you cannot take

anything. Nothing is given, nothing is taken in reality. But still you may have the idea that there is a little more clarity. But it doesn't make you more. So, enjoy the clarity which may be there because it will be gone anyway. Wel-come, wel-go. It's not too bad, but not so good either. It's like a dance. You don't dance to become more, you just enjoy the dance.

Q [Another visitor]: What you say, I accept...

K: No. You will never accept that and you don't need to accept that. You are That anyway; with and without your acceptance. You have to accept that your acceptance will never be good enough. You can accept or not, no one needs it anyway. If you understand it or not, existence really gives a shit about it. Never needs it. This total irrelevance; that I would call is what-you-are. You have nothing to give to this existence and nothing to take away and it will never give you something. Grace doesn't know you and for sure, it never needs you to change. It never asked you for anything.

And that whatever you think existence asked you, for sure is another relative bullshit existence that needs you to be different. Who would that be? That's the question. What existence wants you to be different so that existence would be happy with you? It is happy anyway. It is happiness itself. It is ananda. It is not ananda because you understand something or that you behave in a certain way. It is *chit* – inspite of all the shit you know. It is *Sat* – the self, not because the little me's having a higher or lower understanding.

It is absolute independent of happenings or non-happenings. Who the fuck do we think we are that we think that existence needs us? It cannot get rid of us – that's all. [Laughing] If existence would have a choice, there really would be no universe; it would not even wake up. It would just stay in the bliss of absence, in the bliss of itself. That's the question. If existence could help itself, it would stop everything this very moment. That's why Krishna said in *Mahabharata*; if he could have stopped what had started, he would have stopped it immediately.

If everyone of you here would wake up in the morning with a red button which says – Press here to destroy existence; you will never leave that button alone. If that would really work, you would just press that button. Then you forget and say, let me just leave the button and see what happens and you start again from the moment where you pressed the button. The Taoists say that you go to the samadhi of pure awareness, timelessness, for eternity. Then out of the blue an interest wakes up in the awareness and you go back to the market place. You just have to experience yourself in the next moment; inspite of you being in the eternity of samadhi of whatever kind, you cannot miss one little aspect of your experience.

No escape, no way out. You cannot not realize yourself. You have to fucking realize yourself in every possibility. If you cannot help it, you don't even have to accept it, it will happen anyway – with and without your acceptance. Just be that; and you cannot stop it. If you accept it or not; even that is too much. It's always too much or too less. It will never be right. And that is good enough for me. If it never will be right, okay. Then comes the next – next please.

Nothing can please me; that I like the most. That I don't need to be pleased by anyone or anything. Not any sensation can please that what I am. Nothing will ever please me. There is no satisfaction in anything. This dream can never satisfy me. The next will not satisfy me as nothing before satisfied me. I am Mick Jagger forever – I can't get no, but I try.

I like the song sympathy for the devil; because you are that – always present. Without your absolute presence, nothing would happen, nothing ever happened. But you are the presence and the pre-sense and no way out. No one can take that, no one. That's the beauty of it. That what-you-are never needs to take it and that what tries to take it, cannot take it; never. You cannot accept that. The moment you accept that, you are sad. The sadness comes so immensely to you. It's like a wave of sadness and agony that comes if you try to accept that. The 'me' becomes depressed to the bones because it cannot take eternity. It cannot take it, it will never end.

This understanding may kill you – if you are lucky. If not, it makes you totally depressed.

Q [Another visitor]: I got a smile on my face and a good old suffering happening inside...

K: That sounds natural. It makes the sufferer happy because he is safe. What would the sufferer do without suffering? Could he survive?

Q: No...

K: So, you see, he is happy. There is happiness even in suffering. [Laughter] Tricky old bastard. Show me something what is not happiness.

Q: Sometimes it gets very intense...

K: The happiness? [Laughter] What can we do against it?

Q: Shit, shit, shit...

K: Sat-shit-ananda. The ananda that everything is shit. I would rather call it sat-shit-ananda. There is always a little misunderstanding that you think you need to know yourself to be happy. No, it's the happiness of not knowing yourself. Whatever you know is shit. Thank God and praise the lord, just-in-case. Imagine there may be a God, so just-in-case praise the Lord.

Q [Another visitor]: I always come here with the hope that you would give me something...

K: I give you everything but that's not good enough for you. I give you everything by telling you that you are whatever-is and whatever-is-not and you don't have to know that. I give you absolutely everything and nothing and you are still not satisfied. Isn't that amazing? It's fantastic!

I give you all the hope and all the no-hope and whatever you can experience and the whole dream at once and you are still greedy for more.

Q: Coming here is like a relief, like dumping a load...

K: Then on the way back, you pick it up again. [Laughter] Then you come back again and get empty. Then you go back and get loaded again. It's a truck. You are attracted to the emptiness and get empty again and then you go back and load the truck again. Up and down, fantastic. 'Me' and 'no me'; talked away 'me'. I talk you to death. Then you are born again and you pick up everything again. No-collector for some time, then a collector comes back again. Collecting everything, the past, the future because without past and future you cannot survive as a collector. Then the story continues. It's natural.

All of that is as it is. How can you otherwise live in this world without having a story?

Q: We are taught in childhood to search for the deep truth...

K: No one wants the simple truth. You only want a deep truth. [Laughter]

Q: I come here and it's all good and nice...

K: Then you complain that it doesn't last. Then you say that I have to come again and again. You think one day there will be a moment where in coming no one comes and in going no one goes. For me, that's the absolute intention. But I see that would never happen. Many come and for a moment, no one goes. But then the ghost starts again. So what?

Jiddu Krishnamurti complained that after fifty years of teaching, nothing changed. He was really fucked. He really thought he had a truth or teaching to transmit. Then he was really disappointed that nothing happened. [Laughter] There was no consequence. He really tried his best, with the best intention and his words were really good. Then he thought, why didn't anything happen? [Laughter] Then he said, keep my teachings alive; I heard. If you look at his last pictures, you still see fear in his eyes. And he was meant to be the biggest spiritual teacher of all time!

By all his understanding, with the most keen intellect you can get, with the depth of understanding, the fear remained. Then you can say that whatever understanding you can get, cannot save you. Because as deep as you go with your understanding, you fear to lose it again and you expect something to come out of it. And I mean it when I say he was really the biggest intellect of his time. But if that cannot save you, if that cannot bring the fearlessness of your nature, nothing by all the understanding can be changed. Nothing! It never needs to be changed. Fantastic!

If the transmission of wisdom really would have worked for some, that would be hell. If it really could be transmitted, it could be owned by someone, it could be given to someone, that's hell. The very idea of it is hell. And I like it most that it can never be owned by anyone and can never be given to anyone. Never ever.

Now it's Tolle time and even Tolle cannot.

Q [Another visitor]: I think the word here is deliverance...

K: Everyone waits for it and it never comes. Everyone waits for father Christmas; for deliverance; to be set free.

Q: And that's the biggest trap...

K: Yeah. You wait for something to end. It never started, how can it end? But you wait for the end. Deliverance would be the end of suffering. It will never end. How can the dream of separation end? How can the realization of reality end? If it could end, Reality could end as well. The moment realization could end; Reality could end because in nature they are not two. If one could end, the other could end as well. How can that happen?

Keep dreaming. You cannot otherwise anyway. You have to realize yourself. But you will never realize that what is realizing itself; and you don't have to. And you have to realize yourself...

So, welcome to the never-ending toilet. [Laughter] And you know what happens in toilets? Shit happens! This is your total toilet and only in toilets shit happens. In your living room; it's a rumour.

And you have room-mates in the living room. Then she thinks how can he laugh about it? I hate my room-mates, especially the one who wakes up in the morning. [Laughter] The one who always needs room; this little rumour who wakes up in the morning.

Thank you for going. [Laughter]

January 5, 2014
Mumbai, India

www.ingramcontent.com/pod-product-compliance
Lightning Source LLC
Chambersburg PA
CBHW050556170426
43201CB00011B/1710